EXPLORING MID-AMERICA

Hippocrene USA Guide to
EXPLORING
MID-AMERICA
A Guide to Museum Villages

Gerald L. Gutek
and
Patricia A. Gutek

HIPPOCRENE BOOKS
New York

For information, address
Hippocrene Books, Inc.
1711 Madison Ave.
New York, NY 10016

Library of Congress Cataloging-in-Publication Data

Gutek, Gerald Lee.
  Exploring mid-America : a guide to museum villages / Gerald L.
Gutek and Patricia A. Gutek.
    p. cm.
  ISBN 0-87052-643-X
  1. Middle West—Description and travel—Guide-
books.   2. Great Plains—Description and travel—Guide-
books.   3. Historical museums—Middle West—Guide-
books.   4. Historical museums—Great Plains—Guide-
books.   5. Parks—Middle West—Guide-books.   6. Parks—
Great Plains—Guide books.   7. Historic sites—Middle West—
Guide-books.   8. Historic sites—Great Plains—Guide-
books.   I. Gutek, Patricia, 1941–   II. Title.
  F355.G87   1990
  917.804'33—dc20   89-26734
                                                                  CIP

Editorial development, design and production by
Combined Books, Inc., 26 Summit Grove Ave., Suite 207,
Bryn Mawr, PA 19010, (215) 527-9276.

Printed in the United States of America.

Contents

Introduction

Discovering America's past is an adventure that can take you in any direction to the remotest corners of our land. Everywhere you look, there are historic treasures that provide glimpses of earlier times and people. Both governmental agencies, like the National Park Service, and private citizens who form local historical groups have preserved, restored and interpreted important sites that reveal our roots.

In this volume, we explore Mid-America, a region defined as west of the Mississippi River but in America's interior, not along the coast. It is the near West, part of the western frontier that witnessed pioneers in covered wagons, Indians being relocated to accommodate the white man's thirst for land, and the inevitable wars between native people and soldiers from frontier army forts.

Westward settlement across the Great Plains followed the Oregon, the Morman, and the Sante Fe trails as American pioneers from the East crossed the continent on foot and in wagon trains. But the Great Plains region itself was really the last frontier of America as this so-called "Great American Desert" did not attract many settlers until the mid-1800s. The Civil War, the Homestead Act of 1862 which offered land to settlers, and the construction of the railroad spurred the movement of land-hungry white settlers into territory that had been the province of the Plains Indians.

The outdoor museum villages in the Plains states depict the frontier of the sod buster and farmer, represented at the Living History Farms at Des Moines, Iowa; the Stuhr Museum of the Prairie Pioneer at Grand Island, Nebraska; and Bonanzaville at West Fargo, North Dakota.

An important and colorful part of the territory's history was the presence of the U.S. Army, the infantry and cavalry units, that garrisoned the string of forts erected along the westward trails. First established to protect the travelers, the forts often became trading posts, helped to keep peace with the Indians, offered protection to railroad construction crews, helped to keep white settlers from encroaching on Indian lands, and in some cases became Indian agencies. The military history of Mid-America is preserved and comes alive at Fort Robinson, Crawford, Nebraska; at Fort Gibson, Oklahoma; and at Fort Snelling, St. Paul, Minnesota.

The cultures of the Indian tribes that were contemporary with the settlement of Mid-America, the Cherokees and the Plains Indians, are described in the sections on Tsa-La-Gi Indian villages at Tahlequah and Indian City, U.S.A., at Andarko in Oklahoma.

Exploring Mid-America: A Guide to Museum Villages, is a guide to some of the best outdoor museums which portray aspects of the rich history of the area. The focus of this book is the outdoor museum because it best captures the mood and flavor of the Mid-West since its buildings and artifacts are located in the natural settings that are characteristic of the region.

We define an outdoor museum as an excavated, restored, or recreated assemblage of significant dwellings, buildings, or archeological ruins located in a contiguous fashion, in a site that is open to the public either free or for an admission charge. We exclude historic districts where the buildings may not be open to the public, indoor museums, isolated historic buildings, and historical markers which designate the place where an important historical event occurred but where physical historic remnants no longer exist.

Our book is intended to be a usable guide to significant museum villages of Mid-America. It is designed to help you plan your travel, to provide an accurate historical interpretation of the site, to identify and describe the major buildings that you will visit on your tour, and to supply information about accommodations and places of interest, or side trips, near the site.

We have divided the Mid-American region into two sections: the upper Great Plains states consisting of Iowa, Kansas, Minnesota, Nebraska, North Dakota, and South Dakota, and the lower Great Plains states of Arkansas, Oklahoma, and Texas. This regional organization plan will help you incorporate visits to historical sites with trips to other places of natural, scenic, or cultural interest.

We provide the information that you will need to plan a visit to a particular outdoor museum including its address, telephone number, location, the days and hours when it is open to the public, and admission fees. In addition, we indicate if restaurants, shops, and other facilities are available on the site.

Since travelers may wish to stay near the site, information is provided on overnight accommodations in nearby inns, hotels, motels, and campgrounds. Although we have made every effort to keep this information current, some changes may have occurred since the publication of this book. You might want to call ahead if you have questions.

As is true of any kind of travel, knowledge about the place

that you are visiting will enrich your experience. Historical traveling enables you to be a traveler in time. Outdoor museums, in particular, provide a kind of total immersion in the past. For each museum village in the book, we include a section on its history that will orient you to the site. Here, we comment on the persons who lived at the location and the important events that took place there. We also briefly comment on the process of archeological excavation and/or historical restoration or re-creation that was used to develop the site into an outdoor museum.

In addition to reading our history of the sites, we suggest that you avail yourself of the orientation that may be found on the sites. Many sites, especially those that are National Parks and Monuments, have excellent slide or video presentations. Spending a few minutes viewing such a presentation is a great help in understanding and appreciating the history and significance of the site. Maps and detailed guidebooks may also be available in the visitors' center, which should be your first stop.

After you have oriented yourself to the site and its history, the book's section called the "Tour" will take you through the major buildings found in the particular outdoor museum. Here, we describe the building, identify it by type and structure, tell you who lived in it, describe its interior and relate it to the whole village, town, or community. While some of the outdoor museums have guided tours or docents to explain the buildings and artifacts on the site, most of them rely on the self–guided tour. The tour that we provide gives you the essential information that you need for the self-guided tour.

We would like to thank and commend the United States National Park Sevice, which is responsible for protecting and preserving America's history. Too much praise can not be given to this department which provides tourists with the finest vacation destinations America has to offer, our favorites being those extraordinary sites that combine incredible scenery with fascinating history.

We have written *Exploring Mid-America* so that you can

join us as time travelers in re-experiencing a fascinating and important part of our country's heritage. We hope that our book will help you to enjoy the American heritage as much as we have.

Gerald and Patricia Gutek

PART I

UPPER GREAT PLAINS

1

IOWA

Amana Colonies

German Inspirationist communal colonies from 1854 to 1932

ADDRESS: Amana Colonies Travel Council, Box 9, Amana, IA, 52203
TELEPHONE: (319) 622-3828
LOCATION: Off I-80, exit 225, S.R. 149 to U.S. 6
OPEN: Daily, year round. Hours and dates for specific museums are provided in the section on the tour.
ADMISSION: Specific information for various museums is provided in the section on the tour.
FACILITIES: Many restaurants featuring German cuisine; craft shops, wineries, bakeries, furniture shops, and a woolen mill; colony tours
HOTELS/MOTELS: Amana Holiday Inn, P.O. Box 187, Amana 52203, tel. (319) 668-1175; Best Western Colony Haus Motor

Inn, R.R. 2, Williamsburg 52361, tel. (319) 668-2097
INNS: Die Heimat Country Inn, Homestead 52236, tel. (319)
622-3937
CAMPING: Hannen Park, P.O. Box 244, Vinton 52349, tel.
(319) 454-6382; Kent Park, R.R. 2, Oxford 52322, tel. (319)
645-2315

History

Iowa is a gateway state to the country's western regions.
Travelers who are heading to the Rocky Mountains and other
national parks and scenic areas in the western states often cross
the Mississippi River, enter Iowa, and go westward over Interstate 80. As you travel westward through Iowa, you will encounter the Amana Colonies near Iowa City.

Established by German immigrants who left the Old World
to find religious freedom in the New, the Amana Colonies are
a testament to America's ethnic and religious diversity. Each
year thousands of travelers visit the seven colonies of Amana,
West Amana, High Amana, Middle Amana, East Amana,
South Amana, and Homestead that are known collectively as
the Amana Colonies. Especially in the summer and autumn,
the Amana Colonies are bustling with tourists who are shopping for sturdy and warm Amana woolens and skillfully made
handicrafts or enjoying hearty German food served family
style in the many local restaurants. While good food and
shopping are part of the Amana experience, a visit to the
Amana Colonies is enriched by a perspective into their rich
cultural and religious heritage and traditions.

The Amana Colonies were settled in 1854 by the "True
Inspirationists," a German religious sect. Not to be confused
with other small denominations such as the Amish and
Shakers, the Inspirationists are a distinct religious group.

The Amana story really began in 1714 in southwestern
Germany when two "inspired persons," called *Werkzeuge* in
their native Germany, began to receive what they believed

were messages from God. Johann Friedrich Rock, son of a Lutheran minister, and Eberhard Ludwig Gruber, a Lutheran clergyman, the two *Werkzeuge*, attracted a small flock who believed that God, as in the time of the Old Testament prophets, was revealing his truths to the inspired ones. Because of their emphasis on divine inspiration, the group called itself "The Community of True Inspiration." Essentially, the Inspirationists wanted to return to simpler and purer religious practices that they found lacking in the more formal and ritualized established churches.

Because they dissented from the established Lutheran Church, the Inspirationists were persecuted in Germany. Despite their oppression, the Inspirationists struggled to keep their faith alive. In 1817, the small group of believers was reinvigorated by a revival led by Christian Metz and Barbara Heinemann, two principal leaders in a new generation of "inspired ones."

To escape further persecution by the authorities, the Inspirationists determined to immigrate to the United States. In the 1840s, the first wave of Inspirationists established communities near Buffalo, New York.

In the 1850s the Inspirationist leaders decided to relocate their followers in Iowa's fertile agricultural plains. Amana, the first colony, was established in 1855. Soon, its sister colonies—West Amana, South Amana, High Amana, Middle Amana, and Homestead—were established. Each colony was a small agricultural village which resembled those in Europe rather than the typical individual farm of the United States.

Until 1932 the Inspirationists lived communally with work being shared by all members of the group and property held in common. Unlike the traditional American farm with its individual house, barn, and outbuildings, the Amana Colonies were communal villages where the members lived together and went out to labor in the fields, pastures, and mills.

As a group of colonies, the Amanas were governed by a Grand Council of thirteen elders. Each individual colony also had a committee of village elders who made the decisions for that colony and determined the work assignments for its residents. Agriculture was the primary occupation, with the chief crops being corn, oats, wheat, potatoes, and hay. At their height, the Amana colonists had 25,654 acres under intensive cultivation.

The Amana Colonies became well known for their high-quality woolens, furniture, and other handicraft products. The manufacture and sale of these items as well as the processing of delicious grape and fruit wines remain a major feature of the colonies that attracts many visitors.

Each colony had a blacksmith's shop, a cabinetmaker's shop, a general store, post office, bakery, dairy, winery, and sawmill. The major industry in Amana and Middle Amana was the woolen mill, still operating today, which manufactured the durable warm cloth for which the colony is famous. Visitors to the Amanas can see many of these crafts being practiced—not as museum demonstrations—but to produce items for sale.

Each of the seven colonies was designed following standards of practicality and utility. From the village main street, a series of smaller side streets led to large buildings that housed the communal kitchens and dining rooms. Instead of having individual kitchens for each household, food was prepared in large communal kitchen houses by teams of ten women, supervised by a *kuchenbas*, or kitchen boss. In the large dining rooms of these houses, as many as forty persons gathered for their meals.

Most of the Inspirationists lived in communal houses, which were made of sandstone, brick, or unpainted wood. Without kitchens, these houses contained a central hall, with two two-room suites on each floor. A distinctive feature of the exterior of the buildings are the trellises, covered with grapevines, that are located on their walls. The grapevines not only provided a natural insulation but also produced the grapes from which the delicious Amana wines were made.

Although the Inspirationists were and still are an intensely religious people, often attending eleven church services each week, visitors may have difficulty locating the colony churches. Unlike other Christian churches with steeples and crosses, the simple stone or brick Inspirationist churches resemble elongated houses, with the elders' residences located at the ends. Each church has two or more meeting rooms, the largest of which is used for the general religious services. Church interiors are rather austere but peaceful, with the walls painted a pale blue and dark wood floors. With the congregation seated on hard, plain wooden benches, the general worship service consisted of Scripture readings, the recorded testimonies of the "inspired" *Werkzeuge*, and the singing of hymns.

One of the major reasons why the Inspirationists left Germany was to have the freedom to educate their children according to their religious beliefs. The schools that they developed were designed not only to educate the colonies' children but to free mothers from child-rearing tasks so that they could serve in other occupations. From age two to seven, children attended the *kinderschule*, or children's school. Similar to a kindergarten, the *kinderschule* provided both day care and early childhood education under the supervision of young women who were assigned to the school as teachers. From age seven to fourteen, children attended colony schools that taught reading, writing, and arithmetic as well as the Inspirationist religious values and work ethic. Some young people attended high school outside of the colony, and a few of them were designated by the elders to receive a college education so that they could be of service to the colonies.

In 1932, during the Great Depression, the colonies experienced what is called the "great change" from communal ownership to private property. After much deliberation, the Grand Council proposed to reorganize the economy of the colonies on the basis of private ownership. When the question was put to a vote, more than 90 percent of the colonists voted for the change to private ownership.

Today, the colonies are communities in which many of the residents are descendants of the original Inspirationists who came to Iowa in search of religious freedom. Many of the buildings that remain reflect the craftsmanship of the carpenters who built them to last.

Tour

When you tour the Amana Colonies, you should visualize them in two dimensions: as a whole and as separate units or communities. The seven colonies together form a whole way of life that originally was organized according to Inspirationist religious beliefs and the inherited and transplanted traditions of nineteenth-century rural Germany. Each colony also should be viewed as a close-knit agricultural village with its own stores, shops, wineries, and restaurants that reflect the Amana ethnic tradition.

The **Museum of Amana History,** in the village of Amana, is maintained by the Amana Heritage Society, a nonprofit organization dedicated to preserving the Amana cultural tradition. It is open from 10 A.M. to 5 P.M. daily and from 12 NOON to 5 P.M. on Sundays, from April 15 to November 15. Admission is $2 for adults and 75 cents for children from 6–14. For additional information, contact the Amana Heritage Society, Amana, IA 52203, tel. (319) 622-3567.

In this museum complex, the documents, artifacts, and other items of the Amana heritage are preserved and exhibited. A visit to the museum should be the first stop on your tour. A slide presentation in the museum's schoolhouse auditorium provides a useful orientation to the Amana Colonies and their history. A guided tour of the museum is also available.

The museum complex consists of several buildings: the **Noe House,** the **Village Schoolhouse,** and the **washhouse** and **woodshed.** Built in 1864, the Noe House features exhibits on the Inspirationist religion, a replica of the Amana church, heirlooms donated by Amana families, artifacts, tools, and utensils. Of special interest is an exhibition of Prestele lithographs, particularly of fruits, flowers, and vegetables.

The Amana Schoolhouse, which was an active school from 1870–1955, is now an information and publications center. It also contains a classroom, a tailor and sewing shop, a *kinderschule*, and exhibits of Amana toys and handicraft items. The washhouse and woodshed feature exhibits of tools, farm implements, and baskets. The Amana baskets, especially those made of coiled and split oak, are of special interest to collectors.

The **Amana Artists Guild Community Arts Center,** in High Amana, is located in a community building that was constructed in 1856. It is maintained by the guild, a nonprofit organization dedicated to preserving Amana's artistic heritage, especially in handicraft products. The art gallery features rotating exhibits of early Amana art, folk art, and crafts. The guild also publishes descriptive booklets on such Amana crafts as basketmaking, fiber art, tinsmithing, and lawn art. For further information, write to the Amana Artists Guild, Box 114, Amana, IA 52203.

The **Amana Heim,** featuring the **Amana Home and Blacksmith Shop Museum,** in Homestead, one of the Amana Colonies, is open daily from 10 A.M. to 5 P.M. and from 12 NOON to 5 P.M. on Sundays from April to November. The Amana Heim is a century-old, eight-room brick house. Its interior, painted in the favorite light blue of the Amanas, contains exhibits of furniture, antiques, and other items associated with the colonies. There is also an exhibit of children's dolls, toys, and furniture. Near the house is a blacksmith shop with hearth, forge, and tools. For additional information, write to the Amana Home and Blacksmith Shop Museum, Homestead, IA, 52236, tel. (319) 622-3976.

In addition to the historic sites mentioned above, the Amana colonies have many craft shops, wineries, specialty stores, and restaurants. While all of these establishments cannot be mentioned here, the following are identified as uniquely exemplifying the Amana tradition.

The **Amana Bread and Pastry Shop** in Amana features items from the Amana Society bakery. The **Amana Meat Shop and Smoke House** is an old-time butcher shop specializing in locally produced ham, bacon, sausages, and cheese. The **Original Amana Furniture and Clock Shop** contains a workshop and display rooms with walnut, cherry, and oak furniture crafted by the Guild of Amana Cabinetmakers. The **Amana Woolen Mill** provides guided tours; among its products are yard goods, blankets, robes, sweaters, jackets, and coats.

The **West Amana Store,** built in 1863 in West Amana, is a restored sandstone structure. It features antiques, quilts, folk art, and other items made by local craftspeople.

In Middle Amana, the **Kraus Old Style Colony Winery** produces naturally fermented wines made from fruit, berries, vegetables, and blossoms. Also in Middle Amana is **Hahn's Hearth Oven Bakery** where breads and cakes are baked in an original wood-fired oven.

In South Amana, the **Brumwell Flour Mill** produces stoneground wheat, corn, oats, rye, and buckwheat flours. The **Barn** has displays of farm equipment and tools of the early Amana period and a display of Henry Moore's "Amana and Americana in Miniature."

Side Trips

An interesting side trip is the **Herbert Hoover National Historic Site,** P.O. Box 607, West Branch, IA 52358, tel. (319) 643-2541. The Hoover site, museum, and presidential library, located three-quarters of a mile north of I-80, at exit 63, is open daily from 8 A.M. to 5 P.M., with the exception of New Year's Day, Thanksgiving, and Christmas.

Herbert Clark Hoover was born on August 10, 1874, in

West Branch. He had a distinguished career as a mining engineer and politician. He served as food administrator during World War I. From 1921–28, Hoover was secretary of commerce in the Harding and Coolidge administrations. In 1928, he was the Republican nominee for president and was elected. From March 4, 1929, until March 3, 1933, Hoover served as president of the United States. His term in office coincided with the Great Depression of the 1930s. He died on October 20, 1964, and was buried in West Branch.

Visitors to the Hoover site can tour his family home, the Friend's meetinghouse, and the grave site. In addition, the presidential library and museum has excellent exhibits on Hoover's career as a mining engineer, government official, presidential candidate, and president. The library contains manuscripts and documents relating to President Hoover.

Living History Farms

Re-creation of a 1700 Indian village, an 1850 pioneer farm, an 1870 town, a 1900 farm, and a farm of the future

ADDRESS: 2600 N.W. 111th St., Des Moines, IA 50322
TELEPHONE: (515) 278-5286
LOCATION: West of Des Moines at exit 125, Hickman Road, U.S. 6, on the combined Interstates 35 and 80
OPEN: Daily, May–October; Monday–Saturday, 9 A.M. to 5 P.M.; Sunday, 11 A.M. to 6 P.M.
ADMISSION: Adults, $6; seniors, $5; children 4–16, $4.
FACILITIES: Cafe, craft store, country store, pottery shop, picnic area
HOTELS/MOTELS; Best Western Walnut Creek Inn, 1258 8th St., West Des Moines 50265, tel. (515) 223-1212; Howard Johnson Convention Center Hotel North, 4800 N. Merle Hay Rd., Des Moines 50323, tel. (515) 278-4755; Rodeway Inn,

4995 Merle Hay Rd., Des Moines 50322, tel. (515) 278-2381
CAMPING: Walnut Woods State Recreation Area, West Des
Moines, tel. (515) 285-4502 (from I-35, one mile east of
S.R. 5, two miles northeast on county road); Prairie Flower
Campground, Cherry Glen Campground, and Bob Shelter
Recreation Area, Saylorville Lake, Des Moines, tel. (515)
276-4656

History

Living History Farms is an outdoor museum and agricultural education center which shows the historical
development of farming in midwestern Iowa. The Farms was
founded in 1967 by Dr. William G. Murray, a professor at
Iowa State University and an authority on farm economics.
Dr. Murray wanted the museum not only to indicate the
historical progression of food production but to preserve earlier methods of performing household and agricultural tasks so
that they would not be lost to future generations.

On this 600-acre open-air museum, each farm is an actual
working farm, and chores are completed using both the tools
and methods of the appropriate period. Even the crops planted
and the animals raised reflect the era represented.

The Ioway Indian Village, depicted in 1700, represents
Iowa's earliest farmers. Ioway was the Indian tribe who dominated this region when the Europeans began their exploration
in the 1670s. Both farmers and hunters, the Ioways lived
much of the year in large, established villages.

After the French claimed all the land drained by the Mississippi River for France, naming it Louisiana, they set up
trading posts. The Ioways began trading with the white men,
and artifacts at the 1700 village reflect that fact. The Indians
were the first people to farm the state's fertile land. Their crops
included corn, squash, and beans. As white settlers moved to
the area, the Indians were continually pushed west. Even-

tually, Iowa's Indians were relocated to Kansas and Oklahoma.

The Louisiana Territory changed from French to Spanish hands and then, in 1800, returned briefly to a French possession. In 1803 the French sold the 828,000-square-mile territory to the United States for $15 million, thus greatly expanding the land that American citizens could settle.

The explorers Lewis and Clark investigated the Louisiana Territory from 1804–06. The Iowa region was organized as part of the Missouri Territory in 1812, part of the unorganized territory of the United States in 1821, part of the Territory of Wisconsin in 1836, and officially organized as the Iowa Territory on June 12, 1838.

Until 1833, few whites crossed the Mississippi River into Iowa, where eastern Indian tribes had been relocated and given large parcels of land. The army was under orders to turn back any whites who attempted to settle in the Indian territory along the river.

When the Fox Indian chief, Black Hawk, attempted to return peacefully to Illinois in 1832, his tribe was met with strong military opposition. The Black Hawk War ended in a severe military defeat for the Indians. Generals Scott and Reynolds negotiated a treaty with Black Hawk in which the Indians surrendered to the U.S. government a six-million acre strip of land along the Mississippi River. This parcel ran the length of the present state of Iowa.

White settlers soon moved across the Mississippi and on to former Indian property. Other lands held by the Sauk and Fox Indians in Iowa were relinquished in 1836, 1837, and 1842. Squatters moved into Iowa in large numbers. As many as 10,000 squatters claimed Iowa lands by 1836, a year before government lands had even been surveyed. Settler organizations protected squatters' rights to purchase their improved lands when public land sales began.

In December 1846, Iowa became a state. Population of the state increased from its initial 116,000 to 675,000 in 1860. Iowa quickly became an important agricultural center.

The 1850 Pioneer Farm represents Iowa's early statehood period in which eastern farmers moved west and began to farm the fertile Iowa prairie. The Town of Walnut Hill, depicted in 1875, shows a typical early Iowa town that emerged to provide the services needed by the early settlers. The 1900 Farm incorporates the technological changes that affected agriculture in the prior half century while the Farm of Today and Tomorrow concentrates on futuristic and experimental changes that could affect farmers of the future.

Tour

Tours are self-guided, with costumed docents at each site. You can start your tour in the Town of Walnut Hill or board the tractor-drawn carts that will take you to the farm areas. With a few exceptions, buildings have been moved to the site or are re-creations.

Living History Farms is located on a 600-acre site where Martin Flynn operated a model farm called Walnut Hill from 1867–1906. After Flynn's death, the state acquired the property and operated a prison farm until 1965. The property was then purchased by the Living History Farms Foundation.

One building original to this property is the **Flynn Mansion,** the home of Martin Flynn. After making a fortune as a railroad contractor, Flynn purchased his 1,500-acre farm in 1867 and became a famous cattle breeder. Flynn's house, a two-story, red brick Italianate mansion, was built in 1870. The twelve-room house has a front parlor, back parlor, dining room, and library on the first floor. Ornate Victorian furnishings decorate the house. Walls are wallpapered, windows have lace curtains and heavy drapes, wooden floors are carpeted, and the decorative fireplaces are of Italian marble. Upstairs the bedrooms are furnished with elaborately carved wooden furniture. The grounds around the mansion are spacious and well landscaped.

Walnut Hill is a re-creation of a small Victorian town

which supplied goods and services to the settlers in the area. Many stores have working craftsmen, including the **Pottery,** which produces a wide range of salt-glazed, traditional pottery for sale.

The white frame one-room **schoolhouse** is heated by an iron stove. Students sat at double desks. Kerosene lamps hang near windows and there are maps on the wall.

The **root cellar,** which is dug into the ground, serves as the lunchroom and cafeteria.

At the **cabinetmaker and undertaker shop,** a carpenter explains his work. The Raccoon River Valley Furniture Company has period tools, equipment, and a coffin display. Children are permitted to try to fit into a coffin. The attached garage contains a 1876 horse-drawn funeral coach with glass sides.

The **Dr. W. A. Heck Veterinary Infirmary** contains both the vet's office and the barn to house sick animals. Appropriate tools and equipment are displayed.

There are a working **blacksmith shop,** a working **broom-maker's shop,** a **doctor's office,** a **bank,** and a **law office.** The **Textile Exhibit** displays quilts and clothing.

Greteman Bros. General Store was moved from Willey, where it had been operated by the Greteman family for almost a hundred years. This yellow frame, Victorian building is stocked with original merchandise and reproduction items.

The **Ioway Indian Village** displays a *na-ha-che*, the house Ioway Indians lived in. These oblong dwellings consist of a grid made of willow saplings covered with large pieces of elm or cottonwood bark taken from thirty or forty trees. *Na-ha-ches* were used for sleeping, with children lying on the floor and adults on raised platforms. Food preparation and cooking were done outside where each family had a cooking fire and pit. The metal pots used for cooking were acquired through trading with French trappers.

A typical Ioway village would have had as many as 1,500 people and 300 *na-ha-ches*. While the men hunted for buffalo from May through August, the women tended the gardens. They cultivated the land and planted seeds they had saved. An **Indian garden** has pumpkins, beans, and corn growing. Agricultural tools made of animal horns include the elk horn rake. After seven to ten years, the land would become infertile and the Indians would move to another location.

At the **1850 Pioneer Farm** is a small log cabin with a stone chimney and a shake roof. The one-room cabin has a fireplace where docents cook a noon meal for the employees. Washed and dyed yarn is displayed and spinning is demonstrated. Simple furniture includes a bed with a quilt and a table. There is a ladder to a sleeping loft.

This is a working farm, and men and women go about such chores as tending the garden, feeding the chickens and pigs, repairing the fences, milking the cows, and looking after the sheep. The barn is used for storing grain and tools.

The **1900 Farm** was much different than the pioneer-era farm. It was usually three times as large and was worked with horses rather than oxen. The Industrial Revolution supplied the turn-of-the-century farmer with plows and other tools.

The 1893 two-story **farmhouse** is not log but painted frame. Inside the house that was moved six miles to this site are manufactured furnishings including a kitchen stove for cooking. The pantry contains row after row of vegetables and fruits which have been preserved from food grown on the farm. Instead of a spinning wheel, the farmhouse has a sewing machine. Family clothing has been purchased, much of it from catalogs, as were dishes, pots, and pans.

The large red 1889 **barn** which was moved seventy miles to this site has several horse stalls. Horse-drawn equipment was used by farmers to plow, plant, and cultivate their fields. A horse-powered hay baler is demonstrated in the barnyard. Again, a working farm, this farm has crops of corn, wheat, and potatoes. Animals raised include beef, hogs, and chickens. There is a working windmill.

The **Farm of Today and Tomorrow** features the futuristic

William G. Murray Solar Farmhouse. This experimental house was designed to save energy by using a solar tank and a wind electric system. Modern furniture, sleek kitchen appliances, and interior greenhouses make this an attractive home.

The **Henry A. Wallace Crop Center** contains exhibits on Henry A. Wallace, who was the secretary of agriculture and the vice president of the United States. This earth-covered building has exhibits on farm equipment and scientific food production.

2

KANSAS

Fort Larned National Historic Site

Restoration of a mid-nineteenth-century U.S. Army fort established to protect travelers on the Santa Fe Trail; site of an Indian agency from 1861–68

ADDRESS: Rt. 3, Larned, KS 67550
TELEPHONE: (316) 285-6911
LOCATION: On S. R. 156, 6 miles west of Larned
OPEN: Daily, 9 A.M. to 5 P.M.; 8 A.M. to 6 P.M., Memorial Day to Labor Day
ADMISSION: Adults 17–62, $1
FACILITIES: Visitors' Center with museum, bookstore, and audiovisual program; living history programs in summer; picnic area; hiking trails

HOTELS/MOTELS: Best Western Townsman, 123 E. 14th St.,
Larned 67550, tel. (316) 285-3114; Highland Lodge, 5220 W.
10th St., Great Bend 67530, tel. (316) 792-1731; Holiday Inn,
3017 W. 10th St., Great Bend 67530, tel. (316) 792-2431
CAMPING: The Village Campground, 101 Village, Larned
67550, tel. (316) 285-3261; Becker's Trailer Park, Rt. 3, Box
23b, 1 E. 10th St., Great Bend 67530, tel. (316) 792-5336;
Hodgeman State Fishing Lake, junction S.R. 156/U.S. 283,
Jetmore

History

Fort Larned was established in response to a need to protect
travelers and commerce on the Santa Fe Trail, one of America's most important overland trails from 1822–80. The trail
originated at Independence, Missouri, and ended 800 miles
later in Santa Fe. Millions of dollars of goods like hardware
and calico were hauled to Santa Fe by oxen or mule-driven
caravans, returning to Missouri with cattle, furs, hides, Mexican mules and pesos.

The first explorer to trace a route between St. Louis and
Santa Fe was Pedro Vial, a Frenchman hired by Spain, in
1792. William Becknell brought the first major trade caravan
over part of the route explored by Vial in 1821.

In the late 1840s, trouble between the traders, emigrants,
and Indians along the Santa Fe Trail accelerated because of the
acquisition of California and the Southwest from Mexico as a
result of the Mexican War. The discovery of gold in California and Colorado also resulted in a huge wave of emigration
west. The increased traffic on all the overland trails angered
the Indians who originally occupied these lands or had been
moved there after being dispossessed earlier. They saw the
buffalo herds decrease and the grazing lands ruined because of
the white man's greed and responded by attacking their enemy
on the Santa Fe Trail.

Appeals to the government for protection and military escorts on the trek west resulted in the establishment of several military forts including Fort Larned in Kansas. Fort Larned was founded by the U.S. Army in October 1859 near the confluence of the Pawnee and Arkansas Rivers in south central Kansas. The fort was named for Col. Benjamin F. Larned, U.S. Army Paymaster-General from 1854–62.

Capt. Henry W. Wessells, Second Infantry, who was charged with construction of the fort, was dismayed when he was ordered to use adobe instead of wood as the building material. Adobe buildings constructed included an officers' quarters, a combination storehouse and barracks, a guardhouse, quarters for two laundresses, a hospital, soldiers' quarters, a bakery, and a meathouse. Because of the Civil War, the War Department did not provide appropriations for more substantial structures until 1866. Nine buildings constructed of pine timbers shipped in from the east and sandstone from local quarries replaced the original adobe buildings.

One of Fort Larned's prime responsibilities was defending the Kansas segment of the Santa Fe Trail from attacks by Plains Indians. The fort also cooperated with Fort Lyon, Colorado, and Fort Union, New Mexico, in protecting the Cimarron Cutoff and the Mountain Branch parts of the Santa Fe Trail.

The new fort was the northern anchor of a line of forts defining the southwestern military frontier. This line extended south from Fort Larned through Indian Territory (now the state of Oklahoma) and Texas to Fort Duncan on the Rio Grande.

Fort Larned also served as an administrative center for the U.S. government's attempts to pacify the Plains Indians by peaceful means. In the treaties of Fort Wise (1861), Little Arkansas (1865), and Medicine Lodge (1867), the government agreed to pay annuities to the Cheyennes, Arapahos, Kiowas, Apaches, and Comanches in exchange for not attacking commerce, mail, and emigrants on the Santa Fe Trail. Fort Larned served as an Indian agency and annuity distribution point from 1861–68, when the tribes were relocated to Indian Territory.

Fort Larned personnel were involved in countless encounters with hostile Indians. In 1864, when the Chivington Massacre fomented an Indian war on the Plains, the War Department prohibited travel beyond Fort Larned without armed escort. The fort furnished guard detachments for mail stages and wagon trains.

The Kansas fort was the base for Maj. Gen. Winfield S. Hancock's abortive 1867 campaign against the Plains Indians, which only succeeded in intensifying hostilities.

The fort also was a key post in Maj. Gen. Philip Sheridan's winter campaign of 1868–69. When Cheyennes attacked several wagon trains along the Santa Fe Trail and raided settlers as far south as the Texas panhandle, they caused a general outbreak among Kiowas, Comanches, and Arapahoes, who pillaged and raided from Kansas to Texas. Sheridan ordered Lt. Col. George Custer and the Seventh Calvary south into Indian Territory. Custer's campaign culminated in the defeat of Black Kettle's Cheyennes at the Battle of the Washita on November 27, 1868. This battle ended organized Indian resistance in the Fort Larned area.

Fort Larned contributed to its own demise when it provided protection for the Kansas Pacific and Santa Fe railroad crews in 1870–72. The coming of the railroad with its much faster, safer, and less strenuous service west eventually ended the usefulness of the Santa Fe Trail. The fort created to protect the trail was no longer needed either.

In 1878 the Fort Larned garrison moved to Fort Dodge, and in 1882 the government sold the buildings and land at public auction. The Fort Larned Historical Society initiated a program in 1957 to preserve the fort, and in 1964 it became a national historic site.

Tour

Fort Larned National Historic Site consists of a restored 1868 nine-building fort on a 700-acre site. All of the buildings except one are original and are on their original sites. They were arranged around a 400-foot-square parade ground with a 100-foot flag pole; officers' quarters were on the west, barracks on the north, bakery and hospital on the east, and stables and quartermaster building on the south.

Begin your self-guided tour at the **Barracks/Vistors Center** which was constructed to house two companies of infantry. The restored barracks has a museum, bookstore, and an audiovisual program on the history of Fort Larned and the Santa Fe Trail. The enlisted men's barracks were built in 1866 and included mess rooms, kitchens, orderly rooms, and storage space.

The **Barracks/Post Hospital** was built as an enlisted men's barracks in 1867. It housed 150 men, one company of infantry and one of cavalry. In 1871, part of the building was adapted for use as a hospital consisting of two wards, a mess room, dispensary, kitchen, storeroom, and attendant's room. The east half of the building has been restored as the hospital while the west half has been restored as the barracks for Company C, Third Infantry.

In the **Shops Building,** bakery and blacksmith shops occupied the end spaces. The center workshop area was used for carpentry, wheelwright, tinsmith, paint, and saddlery work.

The **New Commissary** was built as a warehouse to store the overflow of garrison food and subsistence supplies from the Old Commissary. For a while, it served as a hospital annex, and in 1871 the north end was used as a schoolroom for post children and as a library. The schoolroom has been restored.

The **Old Commissary,** built in 1866, is the oldest surviving stone structure at the fort. Built of two-foot-thick sandstone blocks, its south and west walls have gun slits. The commissary was used primarily to store foodstuffs, although the western end of the building was used as an arsenal and powder magazine.

The 1867 **Quartermaster Storehouse** was used to store military clothing, bedding, tents, field gear, and tools. Its two-foot-thick walls also have rifle slits.

The **Company Officers' Quarters** were constructed of sandstone with shingle roofs and broad porticos in front. Each building accommodated two captains and four lieutenants. The captains' quarters were in the ends of the buildings and consisted of two rooms, a kitchen, and a small area for servants. The lieutenants had one room each without kitchens. In 1870, additions were made to their quarters to provide them with kitchens and dining rooms.

The **Commanding Officer's Quarters** is a private residence which may only be viewed from the outside. This sandstone, two-story structure was the only single-family residence on the post. It had four rooms and a kitchen, with servants' quarters upstairs.

The **Blockhouse** is a reconstruction of the original block-house built in 1865. The hexagonal stone building contained a powder magazine, two levels of rifle slits, an underground passageway, and a well. In 1867, it was converted into a guardhouse.

You may take a one-mile walk along the Fort Larned **History Trail** which goes by the sites of many of the fort's original adobe buildings. The trail begins just east of the post hospital building and parallels the Sante Fe Trail at one point.

You may also visit the **Santa Fe Trail Ruts Area,** located in a detached 44-acre site five and one-half miles southwest of the fort. Ribbons of deep-worn ruts from countless wagons are still visible in this native prairie area. Ask at the Fort Larned Visitor's Center for directions.

Side Trips

The **Santa Fe Trail Center** is a museum that interprets the history of the Santa Fe Trail and the surrounding region. Exhibits explain exploration, transportation, settlement, and cultural development along the Santa Fe Trail. Open daily from 9 A.M. to 5 P.M., it is located on S.R. 156, 4 miles east of the fort. The address is Rt. 3, Larned, KS 67550; tel. (316) 285-2054.

3

MINNESOTA

Historic Fort Snelling

Restoration of an 1820s Northwest Territory frontier army fort;
National Register, National Historic Landmark

ADDRESS: Fort Snelling History Center, St. Paul, MN 55111
TELEPHONE: (612) 726-1171
LOCATION: Near Minneapolis–St. Paul International Airport;
use Fort Snelling exits from S. R. 5 and S. R. 55
OPEN: Daily, 10 A.M. to 5 P.M., May–October
ADMISSION: Adults, $2; children 6–15 and seniors, $1
FACILITIES: History Center with museum, gift shop, and film
presentation
HOTELS/MOTELS: Days Inn Airport, 8401 Cedar Ave. South,
Minneapolis 55420, at Killebrew Dr., I-494 Cedar Ave. South
exit, tel. (612) 854-8400; Holiday Inn-Airport #2, 5401
Green Valley Dr., Minneapolis 55437, tel. (612) 831-8000;

Sheraton Airport Inn, 2525 E. 78th St., Minneapolis 55420, tel. (612) 854-1771
INNS: Schumacher's, 212 W. Main St., New Prague 56071, tel. (612) 445-7285; Lowell Inn, 102 N. 2nd St., Stillwater 55082, tel. (612) 439-1100
CAMPING: William O'Brien State Park, Stillwater 55082, tel. (612) 433-2421; Interstate State Park, Taylors Falls 55084, tel. (612) 465-5711; Backstretch R.V. Park and Campground, 8855 13th Ave. East Shakopee 55379, tel. (612) 445-1044; Lowry Grove, 2501 Lowry Ave. NE, Minneapolis 55408, tel. (612) 781-3148

History

In 1803 the United States acquired the Louisiana Purchase, those large expanses of land west of the Mississippi River that had belonged to France and Spain. Interest developed in solidifying the American claim to the Upper Mississippi Valley, which was inhabited by tribes of Indians and British fur traders, by sending exploration parties and establishing military forts.

President Jefferson wanted to establish the nation's presence in the Northwest Territory because a British territorial threat still existed and the northern boundary with British possessions in Canada was vague and poorly defined. He also wanted to assume control of commerce, including fur trading, most of which was conducted by river travel. The explorer William Clark recommended placing fortified trading posts at critical river junctions, including that of the Minnesota and Mississippi Rivers.

Lt. Zebulon Pike and a detachment of twenty soldiers were sent north to the Upper Mississippi Valley in 1805 to obtain permission from the Dakota Indians to erect a military post and trading house at the confluence of the Minnesota and Mississippi Rivers. Pike quickly struck a deal with the Dakotas

for land and the establishment of a trading house in exchange
for $200 worth of trinkets, some cash, and whisky. Although
President Jefferson urged the Senate in 1808 to ratify Pike's
treaty along with an additional $2,000 payment to the Indians,
no fort was built.

After the War of 1812, which effectively ended British
territorial claims south of the forty-ninth parallel, British fur
traders were still operating in the Northwest. An 1816 law
excluded foreigners from trading in America. Secretary of War
John C. Calhoun took an aggressive interest in controlling fur
trading in the Northwest Territory, which included the establishment of forts. Calhoun became convinced of the need for a
fort in the Upper Mississippi Valley on the basis of an 1818
report by Maj. Stephen H. Long, who had explored the site
selected by Pike.

A cantonment was founded by Lt. Col. Henry Leavenworth
in 1819, but it was Col. Josiah Snelling who built the permanent fort on the bluff overlooking the Mississippi and Minnesota rivers. Constructed of limestone quarried from the
surrounding bluff, it was a majestic diamond-shaped en-
closure with round, hexagonal, and pentagonal towers. The
stone construction and elevated site of the fortress contributed
to its castlelike appearance. Labor was provided by the soldiers.

Although initially called Fort St. Anthony after the nearby
St. Anthony Falls, the name was changed to Fort Snelling in
1825 when construction was completed. Outside the fort
walls, an Indian agency was built which distributed government food, gunpowder, tobacco, and whisky and operated a
blacksmith shop. Snelling, the commander of the fort, and
Lawrence Taliaferro, the Indian agent, formed a successful
partnership in dealing peacefully with the Indians.

A soldier's life at the chronically understaffed frontier post
was difficult because of the harsh winters. Food and supplies,
which were supposed to arrive by river boats, were chronically
late and inadequate. Still, there were occasional dances, band

concerts, and formal dinners at the commandant's house, plus hunting, fishing, ice skating, and card-playing. The post even had a library.

Military outposts on the Northwest Frontier had many roles. They were to be instruments of foreign policy which would end British domination of the fur trade by controlling river traffic. Another mission was to keep peace with the Indians and acquire their lands. This was accomplished by gradually gaining their trust and supplying their needs at the same time as impressing them with the army's superior military power. The frontier army was also charged with keeping whites from settling on Indian lands until they had been acquired by treaty. Because of the absence of civil authority on the frontier, fort personnel assumed the duties of a police force. What the military did not do very much of was to engage in traditional military activities.

Snelling left the post in 1827 and was replaced by Lt. Col. Zachary Taylor, who would be elected president of the United States in 1848. Under Taylor served less than one hundred men, and the fort no longer served as regimental headquarters.

Over the next thirty years, Fort Snelling would be commanded by a string of officers. While the military significance of the fort declined, it became the center of commercial activity in the valley. Traders stopped at the fort to have their goods inspected. The American Fur Company and the Columbia Fur Company built headquarters nearby, and their employees and their families settled at Mendota. The Indian agency was an important trading post and a popular gathering place for Dakota and Ojibway Indians.

In the 1820s, Col. Snelling made an exception to the ban on white settlement on Fort Snelling land. According to the treaty signed with the Indians, the land given up by the Indians could only be used for a governmental military outpost and could not be settled or purchased by individuals. Snelling allowed refugees from a failed Canadian utopian colony started by Lord Selkirk to settle around the fort. They built houses and farmed the land.

In 1840 the fort's commanding officer, Maj. Joseph Plympton, forced the Selkirk settlers to move downriver. They settled at Pig's Eye Landing, later known as St. Paul. In 1849 the Minnesota Territory was formed and St. Paul became the seat of civil authority. Now land could also be legally sold to white settlers.

Gradually, the reasons for Fort Snelling's existence were being eroded. Civilization was replacing the wilderness around the fort. The 1851 treaties of Mendota and Traverse des Sioux moved the Indians from Fort Snelling to newly built Fort Ridgely. No longer in Indian country nor on the frontier, Fort Snelling served as a supply depot for newer posts. Land speculators hungered after the fort's forty thousand acres. In 1858, Fort Snelling and eight thousand acres of land were sold to Franklin Steele, a former fort sutler. Steele, who planned to sell the land and start a town, used the fort as a sheep pen.

Dred Scott, a black slave who would be at the center of a famous law case about slavery, was brought to Fort Snelling in 1836 by his master, the new post surgeon. While there, Scott married Harriet Robinson, one of Taliaferro's slaves. Although Scott's owner was from Missouri, which permitted slavery, Scott based his claim to freedom on the fact that he had been brought to live in a territory where slavery was not legal. Therefore, as a resident of a free territory, he was free.

Scott was denied his freedom by the U.S. Supreme Court which ruled that to deprive citizens of their property (slaves) without due process of law was unconstitutional. The Dred Scott case aroused a good deal of sympathy among northerners and highlighted the differences of opinion between North and South in regard to slavery.

The outbreak of the Civil War brought new life to the abandoned fort. With permission from Steele, the fort became a rendezvous and training center for the First Regiment of Minnesota Volunteers. The large fort became overcrowded for the first time: as many as two thousand men were trained at one time.

Ironically, the Indian uprising that was always feared in Fort Snelling's frontier days occurred in 1862. The Dakota Indians, led by Little Crow, took advantage of the troop withdrawals from Forts Ridgely and Abercrombie to rebel. Volunteers from Fort Snelling helped dissipate the bloody uprising. Some of the regiments which had been trained for the Union Army were posted around the state to guard against further Indian attacks.

In reaction to the rebellion, a decision was made to remove Dakota Indians from Minnesota. Fifteen hundred Dakota were rounded up and marched to a fenced encampment near Fort Snelling, where they spent the winter of 1863. In spring, they were shipped to a new reservation on the Missouri River. Companies assigned to Fort Snelling spent the next two years rounding up any remaining Dakota.

In 1871 the government negotiated a deal with Steele by which it would re-acquire the fort and fifteen hundred acres while Steele would receive the remaining sixty-five hundred acres.

Fort Snelling had more lives to live. In 1866 it was designated the headquarters for the Department of the Dakota, which spanned Minnesota, Dakota Territory, most of Montana Territory, and more than a dozen forts. Additional facilities were built for the Department of the Dakota in 1881 on the bluff west of the old fort. In 1889, new barracks were built outside the fort walls to house the newly assigned Third Infantry while the old fort was used only as an ordnance depot. The fort was abandoned in the mid-1890s.

Because of a congressional proposal to rebuild U.S. military posts, the Fort Snelling military reservation was expanded in 1905 and used to house a brigade consisting of a cavalry squadron, two batteries of field artillery, and a full regiment of infantry. National Guard regiments sent to protect the Mexican border from 1913–16 were mobilized at Fort Snelling. Guard units were also mobilized there during World War I, and it was used as an officers' training camp. In 1918, it was designated a general reconstruction hospital for wounded World War I veterans.

In 1921, Fort Snelling became the home of the Third Infantry, and an Air National Guard squadron was based at an adjoining airfield. Later the fort was used for a Citizens' Military Training Camp.

In addition to the Third Infantry, other troops destined to fight in World War II were trained at Fort Snelling, which was also used as an induction center and a Japanese language and intelligence school.

After World War II the Veterans Administration Hospital remained, but an expansion of the metropolitan airport cut into Fort Snelling's property. The fort was abandoned and the flag lowered on October 14, 1946.

A 1956 proposal to encircle the fort's round tower with an expressway cloverleaf was the catalyst which finally led to the preservation and restoration of the Minnesota landmark. A few clumsy restoration efforts had been made earlier. Now, however, the Minnesota Historical Society conducted archeological investigations and began painstaking restoration. In 1960 the site was declared a National Historic Landmark. In 1961 the Minnesota State Legislature created the 2,500-acre Fort Snelling State Park.

Tour

Fort Snelling is an extraordinary find. It's a citadel—a castle-on-the-Rhine structure—a western frontier fort situated in the placid midwestern twin cities of Minneapolis-St. Paul. The fort is not simply located near the cities but is in them, situated adjacent to a large international airport and surrounded by city expressways.

As early as the 1850s, tourists arriving by steamboat came specifically to see this majestic, oversized fort. Having no formal architect, the fanciful fort apparently derived from the imagination of Josiah Snelling, its first commander. Although the fort went through several construction phases, it has been restored to its original 1820s appearance. Docents at the fort are costumed. Playing the role of early nineteenth-century residents of the fort, they perform some military and domestic duties. Living history re-enactments are a regular feature at the fort, and docents are more than willing to explain their activities. The self-guided tour should be preceded by viewing the film about the fort in the **History Center** auditorium. The History Center is a large, modern, underground visitors' center which has museum exhibits, an auditorium, a well-stocked gift and book shop, and offices.

The fort is fully enclosed by a high, gray, stone wall topped by spiked logs. Most of the buildings have been reconstructed with the exception of the Round Tower, the Commandant's House, Officers' Quarters, and the Hexagonal Tower. All of the buildings are in or near the walls, and the open center is the parade ground.

An orientation lecture is presented at the **Schoolhouse** by a uniformed soldier. The school, the first in the Upper Mississippi Valley, was built to serve the children of the military. Officers were permitted to bring their families with them. Enlisted men, many of whom were illiterate, also took classes. The school is a simple, one-story frame building with a teacher's desk on a platform.

The **Guardhouse** is a long, one-story, stone building. Interior walls are whitewashed stone, with wooden trim around windows and doors painted dark red. There are bare wood floors and a large fireplace. The guardhouse has cells for prisoners and simply furnished offices for officers of the guard.

The **Magazine** is a stone, circular building with a roof that overhangs it by several feet on all sides. It was designed to provide cool and dry storage for gunpowder and ammunition.

One of the few original 1820s structures is the impressive **Round Tower,** a three-story, circular limestone building. Walls are very thick and have slits for muskets in them. A circular staircase leads to the observation platform on top of the tower where cannon are mounted and views of the parade ground and fort buildings are excellent.

Luther Leonard Sutler's Store sold goods to the troops and officers. Lists of prices set by the army are displayed although the sutler was a civilian merchant. Goods include metal pots, dishes, cigars, and liquor in addition to furs obtained by trading with the local Indians.

The two **Barracks** housed the enlisted men. The long buildings were divided into many rooms furnished with simple bunk beds with hooks on walls for hanging clothes. There were also married soldiers' quarters and cellar kitchens.

The wooden barracks contain exhibits on the restoration, architecture, and furnishings of the Commandant's House. Another exhibit focuses on the U.S. frontier army from 1823–1903—its discipline, military justice, desertion problems, training, pay, duties, and recreational activities. Muskets and uniforms are displayed.

The **Commandant's House,** one of the original 1820s buildings, is the showplace of the fort. The first floor of this Georgian house has a large entry hall with front and back doors. The parlor and dining rooms are decorated with Sheraton and Heppelwhite furniture, with pewter, china, and glassware displayed in dining room cupboards. There are also two bedrooms, one of which displays the colonel's uniform.

The ground floor of the Commandant's House has a kitchen with a brick floor and a huge fireplace. This level also housed the regimental headquarters in a spacious room with a large table with many maps and other documents. Next to it was the commander's office.

Behind the Commandant's House was a **semicircular battery** from which sentries could watch traffic on the Mississippi and Minnesota Rivers.

Unique to the restoration is the original 1846 **Officers' Quarters.** The first Officers' Quarters, built in 1824, burned and was replaced by this stone building. It features exhibits on archeology at the fort. There is a large excavated area with a narration that explains each aspect of the site. In addition there are displays on changes at the fort from 1821–1902. This building also contains the quarters of the married officers and their families.

The **Hexagonal Tower,** one of the fort's creative features, is original. Walls had slits for muskets and openings for cannon.

Many shops provided the services needed by the troops. The **Shop Building** contains a bakery, a blacksmith shop, a carpentry shop, a wheelwright shop, and a harness shop complete with appropriate tools and equipment.

The fort maintained a **Hospital.** This building is a reconstruction of the hospital that served the fort from 1822 until 1840. The medical facility had a nine-bed ward heated by an iron stove; a dining room with a large red brick fireplace; a kitchen; a surgery with surgical equipment, drugs, and medicines; a storage room containing crutches, wooden coffins, and other necessities; and a steward's quarters.

An extensive exhibit on military medicine, including its diseases and cures like bleeding, venesection, and blistering, is displayed. The post surgeon was also the post weatherman and was required to record temperature readings.

The first library in the upper Mississippi was located in Fort Snelling's hospital.

4

NEBRASKA

Fort Hartsuff State Historic Park

Restoration of a western military post established to protect settlers from Indians, 1874–81; National Register

ADDRESS: Superintendent, Box 37, Rt. 1, Burwell, NE 68823
TELEPHONE: (308) 346-4715
LOCATION: Off S.R. 11, 10 miles southeast of Burwell
OPEN: Daily, 9 A.M. to 5 P.M., April to October.
ADMISSION: Free; Nebraska State Park car permit required: $2 daily or $10 annually
FACILITIES: Visitors' Center; picnic area
HOTELS/MOTELS: Airport Motel, Ord, tel. (308) 728-3649; Hillcrest Motel, Ord, tel. (308) 728-3267; Rodeo Motel, Burwell, tel. (308) 346-4408

CAMPING: Calamus Country Camper Court, Burwell, tel. (308) 346-4729

History

Fort Hartsuff was an army base founded in 1874 to protect both the white settlers and the Pawnee Indians in the Northern Loup Valley of central Nebraska from raids by roving Sioux. The military post was established on the left side of the North Loup River by Capt. Samuel Munson on September 5, 1874, on a site chosen by Brig. Gen. Edward O. C. Ord.

Although its original designation was "Post of the North Fork of the Loup River," the army post was named Fort Hartsuff in December 1874 in honor of Maj. Gen. George Lucas Hartsuff, a Civil War hero, who died on May 16, 1874.

Staffed by a company of infantry—usually less than one hundred men—Fort Hartsuff's soldiers scouted the area in addition to assisting civil authorities in pursuit of horse thieves, murderers, and train robbers.

The height of Indian warfare on the Plains was from 1874–88. The most significant action between the Indians and the military during the fifteen years of the fort's existence occurred in April 1876. Called the "Battle of the Blowout," a detachment of Co. A, Twenty-third Infantry, rushed to the aid of white settlers who were being harassed by Sioux braves. As a result of the battle, Sgt. William Dougherty, a Congressional Medal of Honor winner, was killed. Three other soldiers, Lt. Charles Heath Heyl, Cpl. Patrick Leonard, and Col. Jeptha L. Lytton, received the Congressional Medal for their heroism.

Not long afterward, the Pawnee were moved to Oklahoma and the army pushed the Sioux into the Dakotas. At the end of the Civil War, large numbers of people settled in the region. Since the Indians were no longer a threat to the settlers, there was no longer a need for Fort Hartsuff. The founding of Fort

Niobrara in 1880 also contributed to the obsolescence of the fort and thus it was abandoned on May 1, 1881.

The post was sold in July 1881 to the Union Pacific Railroad, whose intention to establish an immigrant center there was never realized. The railroad sold the property to a local investor, and it was used as farm headquarters. In 1961, Dr. Glen and Lillian Auble of Ord donated the fort site to the state of Nebraska. Nebraska's Game and Parks Commission restored the buildings and incorporated the site in Fort Hartsuff State Historic Park.

Tour

Fort Hartsuff was fairly short-lived as a military base, with an existence of only fifteen years. However, its buildings were well constructed and have survived. The portion of the original 1,280-acre military reservation preserved in the state historic park has nine of the original buildings. They were constructed of grout, a mixture of gravel, lime, and cement similar to concrete. Some former temporary fort structures and the fort cemetery are on private property.

The structures at this small, serene post are arranged around a large parade ground that has a flag pole. The buildings are beige with dark brown roofs and surrounded by white picket fences. The atmosphere is quiet, fairly isolated, historic, and orderly.

Start your self-guided tour at the **Post Headquarters Office Building,** which houses the small Visitors' Center and two offices furnished with desks and chairs.

The **Enlisted Men's Barracks** is a long, one-story building with a front porch. Most of the interior space is a single room with a bare wooden floor, white plaster walls, and dark brown woodwork. Because there are lots of white-curtained windows, the room is bright. It is lined with rows of iron and wooden army cots, each with a rolled-up mattress. The only additional furnishings are iron stoves, gun racks, and lanterns which hang from the ceiling. There are Shakerlike pegs for hanging clothes on the walls.

A dining room simply furnished with tables and benches adjoins the sleeping quarters. Behind the dining room is the kitchen with a U.S. Army iron range and a cot for the cook. The first sergeant has a small bedroom off the long front porch.

The **Infantry Officers' Quarters** is a two-story duplex built in 1874 which housed two officers, Lt. Stivers and Lt. Capron, and their families and domestic workers. Each side has two parlors, a dining room, and a kitchen on the first floor and bedrooms on the second floor. These comfortable, well-decorated houses have rugs, wallpaper, decorative wooden fireplaces, and pianos. They were used for entertaining, and visiting officers were housed here during their stay. Officers' uniforms are displayed in a bedroom. One bedroom is called the Calamus Room, and its exhibits tell the story of the town which grew up around the military base but disappeared after the fort was abandoned.

The **Commanding Officer's House** is the private residence of the park superintendent and is not open to the public.

The **Post Hospital** was built around Christmas 1875, one of the last buildings built at the fort. Serving the medical needs of the base, it was both a hospital and the doctor's office. The ward room is a rather large room with white walls, rust-painted woodwork, painted wooden floors, a small fireplace, and hanging lanterns. Eight cots were available for sick soldiers. The dispensary room is where the doctor saw his patients, and a third room is used as a storeroom.

The **Commissary Sales Room and Quartermaster's Storehouse** is a large barnlike building with a dirt floor and open rafter ceiling. Buggies, barrels, wagons, and fire equipment are stored there.

The 100 × 30 ft. **Quartermaster Stables** originally had a

saddler's room, forage room, and stables for forty animals. Only half of the stables were restored while the other half of the building is used for storage.

The **blacksmith** and **carpenter shops** are small, new wooden replicas containing tools relevant to each trade.

A long, one-story building, the **Laundress Building and Bakery,** housed some of the fort's essential services. On the long back porch are hanging laundry and laundry equipment. Nearby on the grass is a large cauldron for heating water. Inside the building is a bakery with huge brick ovens and large cupboards filled with bread racks. The laundresses and the bakers lived here in small apartments consisting of bedrooms and kitchens. The commissary sergeant also has an apartment in this building.

The **Guardhouse,** a small, one-story building, was the headquarters of the sergeant of the guard as well as the jail. The guard detail was housed there during their daily tour of duty. Prisoners who were kept in the tiny cells were usually being punished for drunkenness, gambling, or unauthorized leave. Display cases of the arms used at the fort are in the guardhouse.

Fort Robinson State Park

Restoration and reconstruction of a United States military cavalry fort, 1874–1904; Chief Crazy Horse killed here; National Register, National Historic Landmark

ADDRESS: P.O. Box 392, Crawford, NE 69339
TELEPHONE: (308) 665-2660
LOCATION: On U.S. 20, 3 miles west of Crawford
OPEN: Memorial Day to Labor Day
ADMISSION: Nebraska State Park car permit required: $2 daily or $10 annually. Fort Robinson Museum and restored build-

ings: adults, $1; children not accompanied by an adult, 25 cents.

FACILITIES: Lodging in original fort buildings, campground, stables for visitors' horses, museum, swimming pool, tennis courts, trail rides, bike rentals, theater, gift shop in The Lodge, Fort Robinson Inn Restaurant in The Lodge, chuck-wagon evening cookouts, handicapped accessible

INNS: Fort Robinson State Park, P.O. Box 392, Crawford, NE 69339, tel. (308) 665-2660

CAMPING: Fort Robinson State Park Campground, P.O. Box 392, Crawford, NE 69339, tel. (308) 665-2660

History

The Pine Ridge plains, the area in which Fort Robinson is located, was occupied by Sioux Indians before whites started moving west for land and gold. The Sioux were migratory hunters who followed the buffalo herds. During the 1840s and 1850s, as many as 50,000 pioneers along with their animals traveled west each year on the Platte River Trail to Oregon and California. They destroyed the buffalo grazing lands and invaded what the Indians considered their territory. As the inevitable clashes between the whites and Indians occurred, military forts sprang up to protect the pioneers.

After years of warfare between the Indians and the whites, the Treaty of 1868 moved the Plains Indians off their traditional lands to locations away from the transcontinental routes. To compensate the Indians for giving up their land, the U.S. government agreed to establish the Red Cloud Agency to supply Indian tribes with food and annuity goods like blankets, cooking utensils, tools, clothing, and agricultural implements. Supplies were to be distributed for thirty years and were intended to ease the Indians' transition from a migratory to a sedentary life-style.

The Red Cloud Indian Agency, named after a great leader

of the Oglala Sioux, was built in 1873 on a low bluff overlooking the White River Valley. It consisted of storehouses, offices, granaries, corrals, stables, carpenter and blacksmith shops, and living quarters for the agency's employees. It was surrounded by a high pine stockade. Sioux, Cheyenne, and Arapaho Indians set up camp around the agency. As many as 13,000 Indians received rations there each year.

After a Red Cloud agent was killed by Indians in February 1874, soldiers from Fort Laramie, Wyoming, were sent to protect the agency. When the military set up camp next to the agency, their visible presence increased tension. Soon, Camp Robinson, named in honor of Lt. Levi H. Robinson, who had recently been killed by hostile Sioux, was moved a mile and a half west of the agency to its present location. Eventually, in December 1878, the camp was renamed Fort Robinson and became a permanent military base.

Indian hostility increased when the Black Hills, which were sacred to the Sioux and protected by the Fort Laramie Treaty, were overrun with gold miners in 1874–75. A series of battles between Indians and western military followed. The Sioux, led by Chief Crazy Horse, defeated General Custer at the Battle of Little Bighorn. Camp Robinson troops were kept busy controlling the large number of potentially hostile Indians at Red Cloud Agency. When eight hundred Cheyenne left the agency for a buffalo hunt, the army, led by Colonel Merritt of Camp Robinson, who suspected that the Cheyenne would join hostile Sioux, intercepted the party and drove them back to the agency.

The army spent the summer and fall of 1876 in indecisive skirmishes with the Sioux. However, it was the cold winter and the lack of food which eventually led the Sioux to surrender at Spotted Tail Agency and the Cheyenne to surrender at Camp Robinson in April 1877. Later, Chief Crazy Horse surrendered at Camp Robinson but remained outside the fort.

On September 5, 1877, the Fort Robinson commander had Crazy Horse, who thought he was being invited to a council, brought into the fort. When he realized he was being put in the guardhouse, Crazy Horse resisted and pulled his knife. In the ensuing scuffle, the Indian chief was stabbed in the abdomen. Carried next door to the post adjutant's office, Crazy Horse died a few hours later.

In October 1877 the Indians were moved to the Pine Ridge and Rosebud reservations in South Dakota. Red Cloud Agency buildings were dismantled, and the lumber was carried to the new locations.

In 1885, toward the end of the Plains Indian War, the all-black Ninth Cavalry commanded by Maj. Guy V. Henry, arrived at Fort Robinson. Blacks had only been allowed to enlist in the army twenty-two years earlier as a result of the Emancipation Proclamation.

Indians at the Pine Ridge and Rosebud agencies in South Dakota were swept by a spiritual movement called Ghost Dancing in 1890. It offered hope to the dispirited, hungry, ill, and dislocated Sioux who believed that ghosts would bring back relatives and buffalo killed by white men. White men would disappear forever, and the Indians would return to their former, happy life. Dancers, who wore cloth shirts which they believed protected them from bullets, could make the ghosts appear by dancing constantly.

The Pine Ridge agent asked for military protection for the agency's employees and property because he believed the incessant ghost dancers were potentially dangerous. Massive military reinforcements were sent. Conflict between Indians and whites resulted in the tragic Battle of Wounded Knee on December 29, 1890. Although Fort Robinson's Ninth Cavalry did not see combat in that battle, a few days later it heroically marched a hundred miles in less than twenty-four hours to rescue soldiers pinned down at the battleground.

The Ninth Cavalry left the fort in 1898 to fight in the Spanish-American War. It was replaced by the Tenth Cavalry, another all-black unit, who served at Fort Robinson until 1910 when it was assigned duty along the Mexican border. At that time, the fort was abandoned until after World War I.

Many of the original wooden buildings at the fort had been destroyed by fire in 1898. At the turn of the century, Victorian-style brick quarters, barracks, stables, a hospital, and a veterinary hospital were built.

Fort Robinson was activated in 1919 when it was designated a Quartermaster Remount Depot. Thousands of horses were trained for army use. When additional stables were added in 1927, it became the largest remount station in the world. At its peak population in the 1930s, there were 17,000 horses and mules. From 1942–46, dogs, called K-9 Troops, were trained at the fort for use in World War II.

A German POW camp was established near the Red Cloud Agency site in March 1943 and lasted until spring 1946. There were three compounds, each having a capacity of a thousand prisoners. Many prisoners worked in Fort Robinson's kitchen, bakery, hospital, grounds, and dog kennels.

Fort Robinson was abandoned as a military post in 1948 since cavalry horses were no longer used by the army. In 1955 the Nebraska Game and Parks Commission began acquiring the property for a state park. Adjacent lands were also acquired so that this Nebraska State Park now comprises 22,000 acres.

Tour

Fort Robinson State Park, located in the rugged northwestern panhandle of Nebraska, is a 22,000-acre park surrounded by high buttes. It does not have a drab, military-base look as many of its remaining buildings are two-story, red brick, Victorian military-design structures that date from the turn of the century.

This historically significant military base has been preserved according to the principle of adaptive use. Instead of restoring every structure to its original use, a half-dozen build-

ings have been restored by the Nebraska Historical Society
while many of the others have been converted to lodging
facilities. The park has lodging for seven hundred guests in
original fort buildings.

Start your tour at the **Fort Robinson Museum,** which is in a
1905 former Post Headquarters Building. Exhibits on Indians
of the region and all phases of Fort Robinson's history fill two
floors. Operated by the Nebraska State Historical Society, the
admission fee charged here entitles you to enter the other
exhibit buildings.

An 1887 adobe **Officers' Quarters,** half of a duplex, has
been restored. It is surprisingly spacious, elegantly decorated
in Victorian furnishings, and even has servants' quarters.
Social life for the officers and their families on this western
base was formal and extensive.

The 1909 **Veterinary Hospital** contains operating rooms,
recovery rooms, and isolation stalls. The horses' operating
table could be adjusted so that the horse could be strapped to it
while standing; then horse and table could be lowered into
position.

The 1904 **harness repair shop** contains workbenches and
tools along with hundreds of army-issue leather straps and
metal buckles that were never used. The shop also contains a
battery chest which was taken along for repairs in the field.
The **blacksmith shop** has four forges, as blacksmiths were kept
busy shoeing thousands of horses. In addition to a tool display,
there are hundreds of horseshoes on poles and in kegs in this
1909 shop.

Nebraska's Historical Society has reconstructed the **Guardhouse** and the **Adjutant's Office,** the site of Crazy Horse's
death. These small log buildings have been placed on their
original foundations. They are typical of the simple structures
first built at the fort that were later destroyed by fire.

In the adjutant's office are the small offices of the commanding officer and the adjutant, each furnished simply with
desk, chair, and iron stove. The guardhouse has the officer of

the day's office and the general prison room. Inside walls are also log, and the wooden floors are unfinished.

The only enlisted men's barracks extant is a two-story, red brick building with white wooden porches running the width of each floor. Called **The Lodge,** it is used as a hotel and has a restaurant, Fort Robinson Inn, on the first floor. Its high-ceilinged bedrooms are simply furnished, and walls are decorated with portraits of famous Fort Robinson personnel.

Travel a mile and a half to the site of the Red Cloud Agency and the World War II German prisoner-of-war camp. No buildings remain. American history classes rarely mention that, although World War II was not fought on American soil, Americans did capture and imprison enemy military personnel in the United States. The museum staff said that former POWs have returned to see and to show their families where they were held captive.

Trailside Museum, operated by the University of Nebraska State Museum, has exhibits on the geology and paleontology of the Pine Ridge and Badlands region.

Rodeos and buffalo stew campfire cookouts are regular activities at this western fort. Trail rides are available. Fishing is excellent in the ponds and nearby lakes. There is even a theater. The Post Playhouse at Fort Robinson is operated by Chadron State College and operates during the summer.

Side Trips

Field trips to the following sites originate from the Trailside Museum at Fort Robinson.

Toadstool Park is known for its moonscape-like badlands and unusual rock formations. The toadstools are sandstone formations and pedestaled clay columns. It is located 20 miles north of Crawford at Chadron; tel. (308) 432-4475.

Agate Fossil Beds National Monument consists of 2,270 acres which contain numerous concentrated, well-preserved

Miocene mammal fossils representing an important stage in the evolution of mammals. It is located at Gering; tel. (308) 436-4340.

Hot Springs Mammoth Site in South Dakota is where Columbian mammoths have been uncovered; tel. (605) 745-6017.

Stuhr Museum of the Prairie Pioneer

Re-creation of a late nineteenth-century Nebraska railway town

ADDRESS: 3133W. U.S. 34, Grand Island, NE 68801
TELEPHONE: (308) 381-5316 or (308) 384-1380
LOCATION: At junction of U.S. 281 and 34, 4 miles north of I-80
OPEN: Daily, 9 A.M. to 6 P.M., May–September; Outdoor Museum closed rest of year; the Main Museum and Fonner Rotunda only open year round, 9 A.M. to 5 P.M., Monday-Saturday, and 1–5 P.M., Sunday.
ADMISSION: Adults, $5; children ages 7–16, $2.50, from May–October. Adults, $3, children ages 7–16, $1.50, from November-April; steam train rides extra
FACILITIES: Visitors' Center, museum, steam train rides, snack bar, gift and book shop, picnic area
HOTELS/MOTELS: Best Western Island Inn, 2311 S. Locust St., Grand Island 68801, tel. (308) 382-1815; Conoco, 2107 W. 2nd St., Grand Island 68801, tel. (308) 384-2700; Erin Rancho, Box 2065, 2114 W. 2nd St., Grand Island 68801, tel. (308) 384-2240; Horizon Inn, Box 1802, 3021 S. Locust St., Grand Island 68802, tel. (308) 384-4100; Holiday Inn-Mid-

town, 2503 S. Locust St., Grand Island 68801, tel. (308)
384-1330
CAMPING: West Hamilton Plaza, Rt. 2, Box 163A, Doniphan
68832, tel. (402) 886-2249; Holiday Campground, Box 1806,
Grand Island 68801, tel. (308) 382-9829; Mormon Island
State Recreation Area, Doniphan 68832, tel. (308) 381-5649

History

Stuhr Museum of the Prairie Pioneer is a large 200-acre
museum complex that includes a Main Museum Building
devoted to the culture of the prairie pioneers, the Fonner
Memorial Rotunda with exhibits on the Plains Indians, a
crossroads railroad town of the late nineteenth century, a
pioneer settlement, an antique farm machinery and auto exhibit, and the Nebraska Midland Railroad, an operating steam
train.
Stuhr Museum was organized in 1960 as a subdivision of
the Hall County, Nebraska, government. It is named for Leo
B. Stuhr, a Grand Island businessman, farmer, and historian,
who donated the land and money to begin the museum.
As a complex, Stuhr Museum tells several different but
related stories of Nebraska's Great Plains. The exhibits in the
Fonner Rotunda convey the presence of the Plains Indians—
the Sioux, Cheyenne, Arapaho, and Potawatomi—who made
their home in central and western Nebraska. Approximately
40,000 Indians were living in Nebraska at the time of their first
encounter with white explorers. The Plains Indians were semi-
nomadic, horse-riding, and buffalo-hunting tribes. In addition, there were the farming tribes of eastern Nebraska such as
the Otoe, Omaha, Pawnee, and Ponca. Pawnee culture is
represented by an earth lodge which is part of the outdoor
museum village.
The next events in the history of Nebraska and the Great

Plains related to their exploration and use as a trail that was
traversed by wagon trains moving westward to Utah, Califor-
nia, and Oregon. A series of explorers, including Captains
Meriwether Lewis and William Clark, mapped eastern
Nebraska in 1804. They were followed by Lt. Zebulon M.
Pike, who explored central Nebraska. Other explorers were
Maj. Stephen H. Long, in 1819; Lt. John C. Fremont, in
1842; and Lt. G. K. Warren, in 1855.

These explorations were conducted under the auspices of
the United States government, which was seeking to learn
more about the Nebraska Territory, part of the newly acquired
Lousiana Purchase. Early reports about Nebraska erroneously
referred to it as part of the Great American Desert, which was
unfit for agriculture.

While Nebraska's fertile soils remained largely untapped
until the late 1880s, the territory's Platte River Valley served as
a major trail road to the Rocky Mountains and the Pacific
Coast. In the 1840s, thousands of migrants to Oregon followed
the Platte River westward. They were followed by the Mor-
mons, led by Brigham Young, who were seeking sanctuary in
Utah. Still more followed the Platte westward lured by the
discovery of gold in California in 1849 and Colorado in 1859.

To protect these westward moving migrants, a string of
United States Army posts was established along the trail.
Among them were Fort Atkinson, Fort Kearny, and Fort
Hartsuff, which can still be visited by modern-day travelers
through Nebraska. Interstate 80, today's trail for the traveler
moving westward through Nebraska, follows much of the
Platte River Valley.

Not all who traveled through Nebraska regarded it as a
desert. Some pioneers, recognizing Nebraska's potential agricultural wealth, saw it as a land in which to settle and establish
homes, farms, and cities. In 1854, Congress passed the Kan-
sas-Nebraska Act which organized the Nebraska Territory and
opened the land for settlement. The Homestead Act of 1863

allowed settlers to claim 160 acres of free land. Nebraska was admitted to the Union as a state in 1867. At Stuhr Museum, a complex of eight log structures from the period 1857–67 interprets the pioneer settlements of this period.

In addition to telling the story of Plains Indians, explorers, soldiers, and homesteaders, Stuhr Museum also features the railroads that traversed and crisscrossed Nebraska's plains. The Union Pacific was completed across Nebraska in 1867. By the 1880s the Burlington railway system formed a rail network across the state. The railroads received large land grants from the federal government to subsidize the cost of construction. In turn, these lands were sold to settlers, many of whom were encouraged by the railroads to immigrate from Europe to America. Stuhr's Nebraska Midland Railroad, an operating steam train, portrays vividly the era of railroading.

An important part of plains life at the end of the nineteenth century was the crossroads village or railroad town. In these towns, such as Stuhr's Railroad Town, a cluster of shops, stores, and offices arose to serve the needs of a growing population. It is at the Railroad Town that the museum's emphasis on community building on the Nebraska plains comes into clear focus.

A visit to the Stuhr Museum of the Prairie Pioneer enables the traveler to recapture the era when the Platte River Valley was a scene of transcontinental migration and then of the settlement of America's Great Plains.

Tour

It is recommended that you begin your tour at the **Main Museum Building** to view an orientation film, "Land of the Prairie Pioneer," narrated by Henry Fonda, who was born in Grand Island. The Main Building, designed by the renowned architect, Edward Durell Stone (1902–78), was completed in 1967.

Stuhr Museum follows the Scandinavian outdoor museum concept in which the exhibits in the main indoor building are designed to introduce visitors to the history and culture of the region and thus prepare them for what they will later experi-ence in the outdoor museum village. The first floor contains an art gallery, gift shop, and auditorium. The second floor, the E. J. Wolbach Hall of History, features exhibits on the 1850–1910 period in Nebraska's history. Among the exhibits are the immigrants to Nebraska, railroading, sod houses, tools and implements, clothing, and a bedroom, kitchen, and living room furnished in prairie Victorian style. There is also a large scale model of the Railroad Town.

The **Gus Fonner Memorial Rotunda,** a structure shaped like a wagon wheel, houses August L. Fonner's (1873–1959) collection of Plains Indian and western artifacts. The center-piece exhibit in the rotunda is Ellis Burman's sculpture, the "Arrow Maker." Among the exhibits in the rotunda are dis-plays on the Plains Indians that include arrowheads, spear points, moccasins, beadwork, pottery, baskets, and buffalo-hide clothing. There are also exhibits on the history of the Fonner family, the horse, chaps, saddles, spurs, lariats, and a western tavern gaming room.

Located southeast of the Main Building is the **Railroad Town,** a re-created prairie community of sixty shops, homes, and offices which portrays life in the Nebraska of the 1880s and 1890s. The next section of the tour describes the principal buildings in the Railroad Town.

Dr. Phillipson's Veterinary Infirmary, a large white frame building named for Dr. Peter Phillipson, a leading Nebraska veterinarian, depicts the important function of maintaining the health of horses and other livestock on the Nebraska farms and prairies. The infirmary includes two operating rooms: one for horses and the other for dogs and smaller animals. Both are equipped with operating hoists, tables, charts, and surgical equipment. A pharmacy is stocked with drugs and medical apparatus. The doctor's office has his desk, diplomas, certificates, and books.

The **Schimmer Barn,** a red barn of the 1890s, contains a display of wagons, buggies, sleighs, and harnesses. It also serves as a livery stable.

The **William Siebler Blacksmith Shop,** a large shop, contains a forge, anvil, and other tools. Demonstrations of the blacksmith's craft are provided. Nearby is the **C.N. Barber Tinsmith and Carpenter Shop** which illustrates these trades.

The **Learned Hose Company No. 1** is a firehouse that contains three large pumps. Nearby is an iron outdoor prison cell.

In the **Town Marshall's Office** is a large desk, cast-iron stove, cot, and clock.

The **U.S. Post Office, Railroad Town,** a white frame building built in 1865, was the home of the first postmaster of Grand Island. It contains postal equipment such as original mailboxes and fixtures from the Merna, Nebraska, Post Office.

The **Millinery Shop** features both women's and men's clothing of the late 1880s and 1890s. Original items, such as hats, parasols, and ribbons, are on display. Reproductions, including a large selection of period patterns, are for sale.

The **Milisen House,** a large gray frame home in the Italianate style of architecture of the 1840–55 era, was moved from Grand Island to its site in the town. Built in 1880, the house has a distinctive hip roof, ornamental cast-iron roof cresting, and wide overhanging eaves outfitted with decorative brackets. The building was the home of Charles and Anna Milisen, early settlers in Grand Island, who came to Nebraska from Pennsylvania in 1867. Milisen, who was an engineer for the Union Pacific Railroad, also served as a member of the Grand Island city council and school board. Furnished in the Victorian style, the first floor has a living room, music room, kitchen, and dining room. The second floor contains three bedrooms. The yard of the house features attractive plantings of zinnias, marigolds, and black-eyed susans. A docent is located in the home to provide information and to answer questions.

The **Leshur House**, a one-story, gold with dark brown trim, frame Victorian home, was built in 1883 by Frank W. Talmadge, a Grand Island building contractor, as his family home. An example of folk Victorian architecture, the house appears to be one story despite having an upstairs bedroom. A prominent feature in its design is a cupola which was part of an early air-conditioning system. When the doors and windows of the house were opened, the rising hot air was forced out through the vented cupola. In 1905, James B. Leshur, a prominent real estate and businessman in Grand Island, purchased the house. Furnished in the Victorian style, the house has several distinctive features. It was illuminated by carbide gas. The kitchen, parlor, and bedroom have elaborately carved woodwork and wainscoting. The kitchen features original stenciling. A docent is present to provide information and to answer questions.

The **Peter's School** is a typical one-room, white frame school that contains a teacher's desk, pupils' benches, and books.

Town meetings and polling took place in the **Washington Township Hall** built in 1884. It now features an exhibit on surveying.

A single, green frame building houses the **O.A. Abbott Law Office** and the **Kenesaw Bank**, built in 1883. There is a display of tellers' stations, desks, and banking fixtures from the Nuckolls County Bank which was located in Nelson, Nebraska.

The **A.J. Sousa Shoe Shop** contains displays of shoes, boots, and shoe-making equipment. The **General Mercantile Emporium** is a stocked general store.

The small-town newspaper is depicted by an exhibit of printing presses, type, and equipment located in the **Platte**

Valley Independent, which began publishing on July 2, 1870. Visitors to the newspaper office can obtain a souvenir edition of the newspaper.

The **Silver Dollar Cafe** is a small restaurant that serves sandwiches and soft drinks. It is the only place in the museum complex that serves food.

Eltman's Barber shop contains a bath, two antique barber chairs, and shaving cups.

The **Pioneer Hotel** contains a registration desk, dining room with two large tables, and kitchen on the first floor; the second floor contains the guest bedrooms. There is a bathroom with an antique wooden tub with a zinc lining.

Dr. M.H. Defenbaugh's Office represents the office and examining room of the small-town doctor.

The **Railroad Town Exchange** features the switchboard of the Nebraska Telephone Company. The telephone exchange was a local business with local subscribers in the town.

The **Fonda House,** birthplace of actor Henry Fonda (1905–82), was built in 1884 in Grand Island. In 1904 the house was rented by Henry's father, William Brace Fonda, and his wife, Herberta. Henry Fonda was born in the house on May 16, 1905. Fonda arranged to have the house moved to Stuhr Museum and restored in 1966. The green frame, single-story home includes a parlor, dining room, bedroom, bathroom, and kitchen. While not containing the Fonda family's possessions, the house is furnished as it might have been when the family lived there. Henry Fonda's last visit to the house and to the museum was on April 6, 1978.

The **Railroad Depot of the Nebraska Midland Railroad** contains the ticket office and waiting room for passengers on the steam train. Adult fare is $2 and passengers ages 7 to 16 pay a half fare of $1. Children under 7 ride free. Passengers can board the train either at the depot or a small whistle stop called Buffalo Junction, which is a short walk from the Main Building.

The **Nebraska Midland Railroad,** a 1906 steam train,

which operates from May through September, provides visitors with a 30-minute trip through the Railroad Town, Prairie City, Taylor's Spur, a buffalo preserve, Runelsburg, and other areas of the museum complex.

Adjacent to the Railroad Town is the **Pioneer Settlement,** a complex of log cabins of the 1860s that includes the **Stelk Chicken House,** the **Bockman Barn,** a **corn crib,** the **Schleichardt Blacksmith Shop,** the **Menck cabin,** the **Schleichardt summer kitchen,** and the **Vieregg cabin.** The settlement is called a "Road Ranche," a place where travelers along the Platte River Valley could stop to buy provisions and have their wagons and other equipment repaired. The Menck cabin, built in 1859, is an excellent example of dovetail log construction. The whitewashed walls of the interior are furnished with authentic period pieces.

Runelsburg, which contains a church and a school, represents a community which was left isolated when it was bypassed by the railroad. The **Emmanuel Evangelical Lutheran Church,** built by Danish immigrants, is a white frame building with green shutters and trim. The white frame, one-room **rural school** contains a teacher's desk, pupils' desks, and large pictures of the martyred Presidents Abraham Lincoln and James Garfield draped with purple mourning cloth.

The **Pawnee Indian earth lodge** is a replica of a dwelling of the Pawnee Indians who once lived in Nebraska. The lodge, which contains clothing, weapons, and tools, is located nearby the Main Building.

In addition to the Railroad Town and its related museum village exhibits, the Stuhr Museum also features an **antique farm machinery and auto exhibit.** Among its two hundred items are threshing machines, steam engines, tractors, farm implements, and automobiles.

When you need a rest, head for the arboretum located between the main museum and railroad town. This wooded area with its flower gardens and a small lake has paved walkways and picnic areas.

Harold Warp Pioneer Village

Re-creation of a Nebraska pioneer village of the 1830s and large collections of inventions focused on the mechanization of the United States from the 1830s onward

ADDRESS: Minden, NE 68959
TELEPHONE: (800) 445-4447; in Nebraska, (308) 832-1181
LOCATION: On S.R. 10, 12 miles south of I-80 at exit 279
OPEN: Daily, 8 A.M. to sundown
ADMISSION: Adults, $4; children 6 to 16, $2; under 6, free.
FACILITIES: Motel, restaurant, and campground
HOTELS/MOTELS: Pioneer Motel, Harold Warp Pioneer Village, Rt. 1, Box 1, Minden 68959, tel. (308) 832-2750 or (800) 445-4447; Fort Kearny Inn, junction I-80 and S.R. 10, exit 272, Kearney 68847, tel. (308) 234-2541; Western Inn Motel, 1401 2nd Ave., Kearney 68847, tel. (308) 237-3153 or (800) 835-7427
CAMPING: Pioneer Village Campgrounds, Harold Warp Pioneer Village, Minden 68959, tel. (308) 832-2750; Fort Kearney State Recreation Area, Rt. 4, Kearney 68847, tel. (308) 234-9513

History

Located in south-central Nebraska in the small town of Minden, Pioneer Village is near the old wagon trail that followed the Platte River and brought many pioneers westward to California, Utah, and Oregon. Billed as one of Nebraska's top attractions, Pioneer Village was founded in 1953 by Harold Warp, a Chicago plastics manufacturer.

Despite his success as an industrialist, Warp continued to

maintain an interest in his boyhood home near Minden, where his Norwegian immigrant parents homesteaded in the 1870s. Warp decided to establish the village when the one-room country school he attended as a boy was put up for auction in 1948. Fearing that the buildings and artifacts of the nation's past would disappear unless an effort was made to preserve them, Warp founded Pioneer Village as a memorial to his parents and to America's pioneers.

Using the theme "How America Grew," Pioneer Village itself grew from its original ten buildings and 10,000 historical items to its present 26 buildings and 50,000 historical artifacts. Since 1983, Pioneer Village has been administered by a self-supporting, nonprofit foundation.

Warp designed his Pioneer Village as a living history museum that followed a deliberate theme—the mechanization of the United States from the 1830s onward. While it resembles a smaller version of Henry Ford's Greenfield Village in Michigan, Warp determined that, unlike Ford's museum, his exhibits would follow the chronology of their invention and development. This chronological pattern makes it possible for the visitor to see the transition in modes of communication and transportation that occurred because of mechanical invention. Visitors can visualize how the ox cart became a wagon and how the horseless carriage became an automobile. While the tours are all self-guided, the exhibits include clearly printed descriptions.

Pioneer Village, located on 20 acres, houses its collection of Americana in many original buildings that have been restored and relocated to the site. Arranged around a village green, the buildings are shaded by a variety of large trees.

In addition to the authentic and re-created buildings, there are several large exhibit buildings. The exhibits begin with the year 1830 to designate the period when mechanization began. The exhibits include inventions that had an impact on homes, transportation, communications, and agriculture.

Tour

The exhibits in the **Main Building** trace the development of transportation, communications, and recreation. The most extensive exhibit, featuring the development of transportation, thoroughly conveys its theme by beginning with an 1822 ox cart followed in the order of their use by covered wagons, Conestoga wagons, stagecoaches, freighter wagons, a horse-drawn street car, a steam train, an electric trolley car, horseless carriages, and automobiles.

The development of the airplane is shown by a duplicate of the Wright Brother's flying machine of 1903; the Glenn Hammond Curtis plane of 1910, which made the first New York–Philadelphia round-trip; and Iowa's first flying machine of 1910. In addition to the exhibits on transportation, there are also exhibits on the development of lighting from candles to the electric light bulb. Other exhibits feature the development of the telephone, typewriter, cash register, and other mechanical devices.

The **Elm Creek Fort,** a log stockade and cabin built in 1869 as a defense against Indian attack, was Webster County's first dwelling and community fort. Originally located at the headwaters of the Little Blue River, the four-room cabin was relocated in the village and authentically furnished. The living room has a display of chinaware; two bedrooms are located in the upstairs loft.

The **People's Store and Post Office** is a general store that is completely stocked with merchandise of the 1880s and 1890s. Among the items on display are high-button shoes, men's shirts, baskets, candle molds, animal traps, crocks, and coffee and tea tins. Of special interest are the potbelly stove in the center of the room, the large bin for vegetable and flower seeds, and the movable ladder designed to aid the clerk in reaching items placed on higher shelves.

The **Bloomington Land Office,** built of Kansas limestone in 1874, was moved to Pioneer Village from its original location in Franklin County, Nebraska. It served as a government land office where homesteaders, many of whom were Scandinavian and German immigrants, filed their land claims after the enactment of the Homestead Act in 1862. It features a display on the Warp family with large photographs of Harold Warp's parents, John Nelson Warp (1847–1907) and Helga Johannesen Warp (1861–1915). Among the other historical documents on display are a copy of Mary Washington's (George Washington's mother) will, an election poster of William Henry Harrison, Whig candidate for president in 1840, and records of land titles in the area. In the center of the office stands a large Simmon's Giant potbellied cast-iron stove.

The **Firehouse and Jail,** a white frame building, features the development of fire-fighting equipment from the hand-bucket cart to the modern fire truck. On display are several pumping wagons and a red fire engine. There is an oil-pumping diesel engine from the Teapot Dome oil field. It also houses an early jail.

The **Lowell Railway Depot** contains the office of the Railway Express Agency, the stationmaster's office with telegraph, waiting room, and storage room. In the railway area are located two steam engines: a wood-burning, narrow-gauge Porter (1880) with a caboose and a larger Baldwin locomotive (1889) which was built for the Burlington and Missouri Railway.

The **Grom School,** School District 13, Kearney County, Nebraska, a white frame building with green shutters, was attended by Harold Warp. Its purchase by Warp marked the origin of Pioneer Village. It is well furnished with educational artifacts and documents such as diplomas, teacher certificates, textbooks, slates, school lunch boxes, water crock and dipper, school clock, baseball bats, and balls. The room, with a corrugated tin ceiling, was heated by a potbellied cast-iron stove located in the center of the classroom. On the walls are pictures of George Washington, Theodore Roosevelt, and Abraham Lincoln. There are also exhibits related to William Holmes McGuffey, author of the famed series of *McGuffey Readers*, and Oscar Warp, Harold Warp's brother, who was superintendent of schools in Kearney County from 1912–16 and the author of Warp's review series.

The sod house is a replica of the dwelling constructed from sod which settlers erected in the often treeless Nebraska plains. Usually they were temporary homes until a more comfortable dwelling could be built. Eleven acres of prairie sod were used to construct the three-foot-thick walls. The white plaster interior contains stove, tub, crocks, chairs, beds, and other period items used by pioneer Nebraska settlers.

The China Shop contains displays of china, pottery, and cut-glass items. Among the items on display are milk glass, commemorative plates, early American pressed glass, "Tiffanized" glassware, colored end-of-day glass, black glassware, Etruscan Majolica, Gibson girl plates, calender plates, and blue willow plates.

The Pioneer Village church, a white frame church, built in 1884, was originally St. Paul Lutheran Church in Minden. It contains a white baptismal font from Denmark which features a large sculptured angel, a collection of prayer books and Bibles, a 1856 Sneltzer pipe organ, a white altar, and dark wooden pews. Sunday services are conducted at 11:30 A.M. from June through September.

The merry-go-round, an 1879 Armitage-Herschel steam carousel, is operational and can be ridden.

The Black Hills Pony Express relay station, Pony Express barn, and blacksmith shop are buildings that give evidence of the era when the horse was the chief means of transportation. The station, an original log building, was the Pumpkinseed relay station to the Black Hills. The barn is an authentically reconstructed building with model horses, saddles, and a 20-team borax wagon. The smith's craft is demonstrated in the blacksmith shop, outfitted with forge, anvil, lathes, and tools.

The **Agricultural Building** is a large exhibition building that contains two floors of displays that trace the evolution of farm tools, implements, and machinery.

The **Antique Automobile Buildings** are two large exhibition buildings that contain autos and trucks, arranged in chronological order of their manufacture. There are displays that show the various models of Ford and Chevrolet automobiles from 1927–60. There are also automobiles made by Willys, Windsor, Frazer, Hupmobile, Kaiser, Graham-Paige, Terraplane, Overland, Hudson, and Packard.

The **Willis Watt Livery Stable**, a two-story barn, houses exhibits of horse-drawn carriages, harnesses, saddles, buggies, sleighs, wagons, a Wells Fargo stage and a Concord coach.

The **Antique Tractor and Trucks Building** contains a collection of tractors and trucks that are arranged chronologically.

The **Antique Farm Machinery Building** houses exhibits of seeding, cultivating, and harvesting machines such as threshers, corn pickers, combines, and haying equipment that are horse, steam, and gasoline powered. Of special interest is the 1910 harvester that required a team of from 24 to 32 horses to pull it.

The **Home and Shops Building** contains exhibits of kitchens, living rooms, and bedrooms that illustrate the development of household furnishings, at thirty-year intervals, from 1830 to the present. Also shown are offices and shops of the periods depicted. In addition to the displays of furniture, there are demonstrations of glass-making, broom-making, and rug-making, with craft items available for purchase. The second floor contains a reproduction of the Washington office of U.S. Senator Carl T. Curtis and exhibits illustrating his career as a Nebraska political leader.

The **horse barn** is a pioneer barn that was moved from the Warp homestead near Minden to the site.

The **Home Appliance Building** contains an exhibit of household appliances such as milk separators, refrigerators, stoves, irons, toasters, scales, iceboxes, vacuum cleaners, and sewing and washing machines.

The **Hobby House** contains collections of dolls, pitchers, buttons, and other items.

Side Trips

Fort Kearny State Historical Park, Rt. 4, Kearney, 68847, tel. (308) 234-9513, located in Fort Kearny State Recreation Area, marks the site of the first fort built to protect settlers moving on the Oregon Trail. Built in 1848, the fort, named for Gen. Stephen Watts Kearny, was maintained as a U.S. military post until 1871. The park's interpretative Visitors' Center has a slide show and exhibits on the history of the fort. There is also a reconstructed blacksmith and carpenter shop and a stockade that marks the perimeters of the fort. The state recreation area has hiking, camping, fishing, and swimming.

5

NORTH DAKOTA

Bonanzaville, USA— Pioneer Village and Museum

Re-creation of a late nineteenth- and early twentieth-century North Dakota village

ADDRESS: P.O. Box 719, West Fargo, ND 58078
TELEPHONE: (701) 282-2822
LOCATION: Off I-94, exit 85, at West Fargo or 4 1/4 miles west of I-29 on Main Ave. (U.S. 10)

OPEN: Monday–Friday, 9 A.M. to 5 P.M., and Saturday and Sunday, 1–5 P.M. from late May to late October. Rest of year, the museum only is open Tuesday–Friday, 9:30 A.M. to 4 P.M. ADMISSION: Pioneer Village and Museum: adults, $3; children 6–16, $1. Museum only: adults, $1.50; children 6–16, 50 cents
FACILITIES: Visitors' Center with gift and book shop, picnic area, Pioneer Review Days third weekend of August
HOTELS/MOTELS: Days Inn, 901 38th St. SW, Fargo 58103, tel. (701) 282-9100; Kelly Inn, 3800 Main Ave., Fargo 58103, tel. (701) 282-2143; Select Inn, 1025 38th St. SW, Fargo 58103, tel. (701) 282-6300, or (800) 641-1000; Holiday Inn, Box 9555, I-29 and 13th Ave. S exit, Fargo 58109, tel. (701) 282-2700; Town House Motor Inn, 301 3rd Ave. N, Fargo 58102, tel. (701) 232-8851, or (800) 437-4582
CAMPING: Cass County Campsite, Red River Valley Campground, W. Main Ave., West Fargo 58102, tel. (701) 282-2000; Lindenwood Park, 5th Ave. and 17th Ave. S, Fargo 58102, tel. (701) 241-1350

History

Bonanzaville, USA, located on the Red River Valley Fairgrounds in West Fargo, is a turn-of-the-century pioneer village that has been re-created and maintained by the Cass County Historical Society. The name Bonanzaville is coined from the large wheat farms that sprung up in North Dakota in the late nineteenth century when wheat prices earned a "bonanza" for their owners. The village consists of authentic small-town and rural buildings that were moved to the site from various locations in North Dakota and restored and furnished.

Bonanzaville recaptures a slice of the history of North Dakota, especially its rural and small-town atmosphere. Although there had been limited settlement in the Dakotas by

Indian traders and soldiers before the Civil War, most of the settlers passed through this region on their way to more heavily forested and better-watered regions to the west. After 1865, however, the free land provided by the Homestead Act stimulated an influx of settlers into the Dakotas. These settlers created a farming economy and society in these plains states. By 1890 as a result of migration from the eastern states and considerable European immigration, North Dakota's population reached 182,719, of whom 44 percent were foreign born. Among these immigrants to the plains were Germans, Norwegians, Swedes, Bohemians, and a unique group of German-Russians. In 1889, North Dakota was admitted as a state. The exhibits at Bonanzaville which highlight rural and small-town life reflect much of North Dakota's past.

The pioneer village re-creates the style of life of rural and small-town North Dakotans in the 1880–1910 era. A Plains state, known for frigid winters and hot summers, North Dakota developed into a fertile and bountiful agricultural region. Among the nation's leading producers of wheat and other grain crops, North Dakota farmers experienced periods of either economic prosperity, known as bonanza times, or of recession with the dreaded farm foreclosures. North Dakota's prosperity depended on the national and world market for its agricultural products. The high price of wheat during World War I especially contributed to the growth of the large wheat farms that enjoyed large or bonanza harvests and profits. During the 1920s, when the rest of the nation enjoyed economic prosperity, North Dakota agriculture, due to surplus, suffered a long recession.

North Dakota's fascinating political history centers around efforts to organize farmers and workers into the Non-Partisan League, which battled against trusts and monopolies and encouraged cooperatives. The heights and depths of a volatile agricultural economy that shaped North Dakota's history can be vividly seen in the restored shops, 'homes, church, and school that re-create Bonanzaville, a prairie community on the Plains.

Tour

The tour, which is completely self-guided, should begin in the **Red River and Northern Plains Region Museum.** The museum houses an interesting but eclectic collection of artifacts dealing with the region's agricultural and community life. For example, it features exhibits on the history of North Dakota and the University of North Dakota.

"Back Street Memory Lane" portrays small-town life in rural North Dakota in 1910 by means of a kitchen, living room, front porch, and parlor which are furnished in the style of the period. There are collections of toys, dolls, a complete miniature circus, miniature farm equipment, Red Wing stoneware, and other items which were donated to the museum by members of the local community.

In addition to exhibits on the Dakota northern plains, the museum also houses the impressive Edward A. Milligan Indian collection. Most of the items relate to the Sioux, who inhabited the Dakotas as well as neighboring Minnesota. Visitors can see such artifacts as Sioux beadwork, arts, crafts, religious and medicinal artifacts, clothing, pottery, bone knives, and other items. There is an extensive collection of photographs of the Plains Indians, especially the Blackfeet and Sioux, some of which were taken by well-known photographer D.F. Barry.

Upon leaving the museum, the visitor enters the **Pioneer Village of Bonanzaville,** which includes the following buildings:

An atmosphere of small-town community spirit is reflected in the **Arthur Town Hall,** built in the 1890s, which was used for graduations, meetings, plays, and other events in Arthur. It was then used by North Dakota State University before being moved to Bonanzaville. Of special interest are its six unique stained-glass windows. Three of the portraits in glass are of William Shakespeare, Henrik Ibsen, and Johann Wolfgang Goethe, who represent the English, Norwegian, and German contributions to North Dakota's cultural life. Other windows portray Congressman Justin Morrill, author of the 1862 legislation that gave federal support to establish land grant colleges and universities; Abraham Lincoln, Civil War president; and the Statue of Liberty.

The **Embden Depot and Railroad Museum,** a well-furnished depot and train shed, houses an original 1883 Northern Pacific locomotive and caboose, a huge railroad snowplow used on the Midland Continental Railroad, an 1930 eighty-passenger Northern Pacific coach, and a 1924 Porter steam engine.

The **Spud Valley Railroad,** housed in the Kathryn depot, features a miniature railroad that operates in a scale model of Fargo in the 1940s and 1950s.

The **Telephone Museum,** located in a hardware store moved to the site from Tower City, illustrates the history of the telephone and its role in linking the small towns of the Plains. A feature of the exhibit is a working telephone exchange as well as a display of switchboards, insulators, and other items.

A **1920s drug store** from Gilbey features an ice cream parlor with a soda fountain and booths. There are also displays of drugs, sundries, and other items popular during that period.

The **Eagles Aircraft Museum,** organized by Aerie No. 153, includes a 1911 Curtiss-Wright pusher, the U.S. Navy's pioneer ship-launched plane, a 1917 Standard J-1, a 1926 Swallow, a 1936 J-3 Piper Cub, a 1973 Pitts Special, a military C-45 Beechcraft, a Douglas DC-3, and an A-26 of World War II vintage.

The **Law Enforcement Museum,** originally the Fargo Auxilary Police Training Center, features displays on police and law enforcement uniforms and equipment.

The **Cass-Clay Creamery,** a replica of a typical 1920s small-town creamery, contains equipment from the Kenmare creamery, the last creamery of its type operating in North Dakota. Among the items on display are a glass milk bottle filler, a cottage cheese filler, an ice cream freezer, a butter churn, and a pasteurizing vat.

The **Page Hotel and Brass Rail Bar,** a large two-story frame building, is a small-town hotel, cafe, and bar that was moved to the site from Page. The first floor contains a reception area and registration desk, a large wooden bar with shiny brass rail, a lobby with overstuffed chairs, and a large Regal Peninsular cast-iron stove. The kitchen contains a coal-burning stove and a sink with a water pump. The second floor contains small simply furnished guest rooms, a larger bridal suite, a parlor, and bathroom. As in other small hotels at the turn of the century, there was no indoor plumbing.

The **Thue and Brink Store,** from Horace, is a general store like those often found on the main streets of small towns in the North Dakota plains. Its large green interior with corrugated tin ceiling is stocked with a wide variety of dry goods, such as clothing, saddles, stoves, baby buggies, sewing machines, and tools. The second floor contains equipped professional offices such as a beauty shop, doctor's office, dentist's office, and chiropractor's office.

In the **Antique Car Museum,** there is a collection of representative antique automobiles, such as the 1903 Ford and 1924 Chrysler.

The **House of Labor,** a small building from Lake Pelican, Minnesota, is dedicated to Henry Martinson, who was a labor organizer, political leader of the North Dakota Non-Partisan League, poet, and historian. It contains a collection of Martinson's memorabilia and writings.

The **Pioneer Fire Company Building,** a replica of a fire station, houses a display of fire-fighting equipment, including a horse-drawn bucket wagon from the territorial era as well as vehicles and items of more recent vintage. On the second floor, a fire department quarters is outfitted with uniforms, cots, a map of the district, and a large pole used by the firemen to reach their vehicles quickly.

Three large exhibition buildings, the **Engine and Machine Shop**, the **Tractor Building**, and the **Farm Implement Building**, contain exhibits that reflect North Dakota's agricultural heritage. In these buildings can be seen an extensive collection of antique tractors, farm implements, threshing machines, and gas engines.

Also illustrating the region's agricultural history is an original 1880s **grainery** and a **farmstead barn**, which provides shelter for livestock exhibits.

The **Houston House**, a large, two-story, white frame farmhouse built in 1881 and originally located near Hunter, was the home of David H. Houston. A Scottish immigrant, Houston, a poet and farmer, invented roll-type camera film, now sold by Eastman-Kodak. Furnished in Victorian style, the first floor contains a dining room, kitchen, library, and parlor. Houston's darkroom used for his research into photography is an unusual feature of the house. The second floor has four bedrooms and a sitting room.

The **Hagen House**, built in 1897 southwest of Horace, was the original home of Martin Hagen and four generations of his family. Never provided with electricity or running water, the house portrays the life-style of many Dakota rural families at the turn of the century. Despite its general lack of amenities, the house is furnished attractively in Victorian style and includes an organ and piano in the parlor. There is a separate summer kitchen.

The **Checkered Years House**, moved from its original location near Horace, gets its unusual name from the title of a book, *The Checkered Years*. The book was based on the life of the pioneer diarist, Mary Dodge Woodward, who lived in this charming old farmhouse.

In the interior of the **District 31 Berlin Township School** is located the **Cass County District Court** restored to its 1904 appearance. The courtroom includes the large judge's desk and bench, defense and state's attorney tables, the jury seats, and a table for reporters. On the walls are large photographs of the judges who presided over the district court.

The **Dobrinz School,** built in 1895, is a one-room school that was originally located in Mapleton Township of Cass County. Classes were conducted in the school from 1895 until 1953. It contains a large teacher's desk, students' desks, blackboards, textbooks, and a display of class photographs. On September 22, 1972, Julie Nixon Eisenhower taught a history class in the school.

St. John's Lutheran Church, built in 1898, is a simple, white frame country church that once served a congregation in the vicinity of Horace. In its light green corrugated tin interior are a simple wooden altar, pulpit, and curved pews. Its large brass chandelier is a noteworthy feature. The church is still used for weddings and other special services.

Reflecting the building techniques of North Dakota's Scandinavian immigrant settlers, the **Habberstad Log Cabin,** a two-story structure, was built in 1874 by Finnish carpenters for a Norwegian family. It was located originally at Kindred.

The **Forness Log Cabin** follows the design of the late nineteenth-century log cabins found on western ranches. It is a one-room cabin, simply furnished, with a sleeping loft.

The **sod house replica** is a facsimile that was erected in 1986 to portray the style of housing sometimes used by early settlers on the Great Plains in the mid-nineteenth century. These earthern structures were temporary dwellings used in regions where trees were scarce.

Fargo's first house, a log and chink structure built in 1869, was the city's first permanent structure. It was later used as the Moore Log Hotel in 1872 and then as the Fargo city jail in 1875. In 1892 the building was purchased by Henry Hector for a family home.

The **Maier Dollhouse,** an 1890's homestead house from Moorhead, houses a large doll collection.

The **Furnberg Store** was a country general store that was

located on the Sheyenne River near Osgood. It is stocked with a wide variety of merchandise, dry goods, drugs and medicines, clothing, and bulk foods. Of special interest are the 1929 Standard Oil gas pumps located near the store front.

The **Hunter Times** is an old-fashioned newspaper office and print shop with displays of presses and type. It is still an operating press that publishes special editions of the village newspaper, the *Bonanzaville Pioneer*.

In the **U-R Next Barbershop**, built by W.J. Frederick in 1900 in Buffalo, is a completely restored barbershop with a large oak and marble antique backbar, two antique wooden barber chairs, a collection of personalized shaving mugs, a shoe shine stall, and a bath stall. Much of the equipment, such as the pewter dip sterilizer, surgical knife, and razors, dates from the late nineteenth century.

In addition, Bonanzaville has a fully equipped **blacksmith shop** and a **harness shop**. There are also outdoor displays of farm equipment and other buildings that are used during the Pioneer Days Review, which is held annually on the third weekend of August.

Side Trips

The Fargo, North Dakota–Moorhead, Minnesota, area has a number of attractions of interest to visitors. In Moorhead is the **Comstock House,** built in 1882 by Solomon and Sarah Comstock and maintained by the Minnesota Historical Society. The eleven-room Victorian House, located at 506 8th St. South (U.S. 75 South), is open on weekends from Memorial Day through September 30. There is an admission charge; tel. (218) 233-0848.

The **Plains Art Museum,** 521 Main Ave., Moorhead 56560, houses works of art by regional artists. It also has collections of contemporary art objects from Native American and West African cultures. The museum is open from 10 A.M.

to 12 noon and 1 P.M. to 5 P.M. from Wednesday through Saturday and from 1 P.M. to 5 P.M. on Sunday; tel. (218) 236-7171.

The **Clay County Historical Museum**, 22 N. 8th St., Moorhead, tel. (218) 233-4604, which houses regional history exhibits, is open from 10 A.M. to 4 P.M. Monday through Friday.

The **Heritage-Hjemkomst Interpretive Center**, 202 First Ave. North, Moorhead 56560, tel. (218) 233-5604, features the Viking ship, *Hjemkomst*, built by Robert Asp. There are exhibits about the ship as well as traveling exhibits. The center is open from 9 A.M. to 5 P.M. Monday through Saturday, and from 12 NOON to 5 P.M. on Sunday.

Fort Abraham Lincoln State Park

Reconstruction of a mid-seventeenth-century Mandan Indian summer village; reconstruction of late nineteenth-century frontier army cavalry and infantry fort buildings: site from which Custer's Battle of the Little Bighorn was launched

ADDRESS: Route 2, Box 139, Mandan, ND 58554
TELEPHONE: (701) 663-9571
LOCATION: Southwest of Bismarck; 4 miles south of Mandan on S.R. 1806
OPEN: Park: open daily. Visitors' Center: daily, 9 A.M. to 9 P.M., June–August; daily, 9 A.M. to 5 P.M., May and September; weekdays, 9 A.M. to 5 P.M., October–April.
ADMISSION: Free; all vehicles must display a state park motor vehicle permit, $2 daily or $15 annually
FACILITIES: Visitors' Center with museum, trading post (gift

shop), picnic areas, campgrounds, nature trails, living history programs
HOTELS/MOTELS: Stonewood Inn, (½ mile north of I-94, exit 31), Box 749, Mandan 58554, tel. (701) 663-0001; Best Western Seven Seas Motor Inn, 2611 Old Red Trail, P.O. Box 1316, Mandan 58554, tel. (701) 663-7401
CAMPING: Fort Abraham Lincoln State Park, Mandan 58554, tel. (701) 663-9571

History

The Mandan Indians are the first people known to have inhabited the area that includes present-day Fort Abraham Lincoln State Park. The Mandans are thought to have begun arriving from the south and east to settle along the Missouri River between 800 and 1100 A.D. Archeological evidence indicates that by 1650, the main concentration of Mandans was centered within twenty miles of the junction of the Heart and Missouri rivers.

The Mandans were sedentary farmers who built summer villages near fertile floodplains of rivers. They lived in earth-covered lodges that could accommodate ten to fifteen people. Lodges were constructed by women in the spring, and construction usually took from ten to seventeen days.

Lodges were supported by four center posts connected by beams which were then surrounded by a large outer circle of supporting posts. The framework of the lodge was finished by extending rafters from the center to the outer circle and from the outer circle to the ground. Then, limber willow branches were laid across the rafters to form support for a layer of grass. Over this was spread a layer of packed earth which was dried by the sun. A hole in the center of the roof served as a chimney and let light in.

The Mandan summer village called On-A-Slant contained

about seventy-five earth lodges. It was built on a terrace which sloped toward the river. Its location was chosen because steep banks along its sides made it easily defensible. In the winter the Mandans moved into temporary villages located in wooded river bottoms.

The On-A-Slant summer village was occupied by the Mandans for over a century from approximately 1650 to 1780. Women tended the fields where crops included corn, beans, tobacco, squash, and sunflowers. The men hunted, traded, and provided security.

European explorers visited the Mandans at On-A-Slant as early as 1739 when an expedition led by a Frenchman, Pierre la Sieur de la Verendrye, arrived. Europeans brought new diseases to which the Indians had no immunity. Smallpox or some other epidemic decimated the Mandans around 1781. The few remaining villagers moved north to join other tribes. By 1804, when Lewis and Clark were exploring the area, only the ruins of On-A-Slant village remained.

In June 1872 a U.S. Army fort was established on the west bank of the Missouri River southwest of Bismarck in Dakota Territory. The frontier fort was built to protect surveyors, construction engineers, and working parties of the Northern Pacific Railroad from Indian attacks. Originally named Fort McKeen for Col. H. Boyd McKeen, who was killed at the Battle of Cold Harbor, the name was changed to Fort Abraham Lincoln the following November.

Built by soldiers, the infantry fort was a self-contained town. Buildings were made of lumber milled at the site or of logs and included officers' quarters, barracks, a hospital, storehouses, a school, blacksmith shop, carpenter shop, bakery, wheelwright's shop, lumber mill, laundress' quarters, and scouts' quarters. A palisade with blockhouses at each corner encircled the fort on the north and west sides while steep bluffs blocked access to the fort from the south and east.

Attempts to provide railroad crews with protection from Indian raids were frustrated by the fact that Indians on horseback eluded pursuit by footsoldiers. Obviously, cavalry troops were needed if the Northern Pacific Railroad was to be completed. A cavalry post was authorized at Fort Abraham Lincoln in March 1873. Seven hundred railway carloads of construction materials arrived, and the post was virtually completed in 1873.

The cavalry post was located on the flats south of the infantry post, and its buildings were larger and more numerous. Buildings, most of which were frame, consisted of seven officers' quarters, a granary, dispensary, guardhouse, commissary storehouse, quartermaster's storehouse, three soldiers' barracks, laundress' quarters, quartermaster's stable, six cavalry stables, and an ordnance depot.

The cavalry base was commanded by Lt.-Col. George A. Custer and was staffed by six companies of the Seventh Cavalry. The cavalry troops along with three companies of the Sixth and Seventeenth infantries totaled 650 men, thus making Fort Abraham Lincoln one of the largest military posts on the Northern Plains.

One of the duties of Fort Abraham Lincoln's troops was to provide escorts for surveying and scientific expeditions. In 1873, Custer and eight companies of the Seventh Cavalry, three companies of the Seventeenth Infantry, and one company of the Sixth Infantry accompanied the Stanley Expedition which surveyed a railroad route along the Yellowstone River. During this expedition, the army had several encounters with hostile Sioux.

In July 1874, Custer led an expedition to explore the Black Hills, an area retained by the Sioux in the Treaty of 1868. Unofficially, the army wanted to check out rumors that there was gold in the Black Hills, but the official purpose was to locate sites for future forts. Angry Sioux felt that the military entering their territory was a treaty violation. The government disagreed, saying there was a clause in the treaty giving the government the right to send its officials on to reservations.

When Custer reported finding gold in the Black Hills,

newspapers quickly spread the word. Gold-seekers soon flooded the Sioux reservation, increasing Sioux resentment. The military were supposed to remove whites who attempted to settle on Indian lands, but the large numbers of whites made this an impossible task. Instead, in the fall of 1875, the government tried to negotiate with the Sioux for the sale of their land or its mineral rights, but negotiations failed.

Although open warfare between Indians and the miners didn't develop, whites were continually harassed by the Sioux. On the advice of an inspector sent to the northern Great Plains by the Commissioner of Indian Affairs, the Secretary of the Interior on December 6, 1875, ordered all Indians to report to Indian agencies by January 31, 1876, or face action by the army. The order was unrealistic because sufficient time was not allowed, winter traveling was very difficult, and the message, delivered by courier, did not even reach remote bands of Indians.

On February 1, 1876, Indians still at large were turned over to the army to be forced into the agencies. This was not viewed as extremely difficult by the military, who estimated that only about one thousand Indians fell into this category.

Because one of the hardest tasks for the army was to locate the elusive Indians and prevent them from escaping, the army decided to converge on hostile Indian territory with three commands coming from three directions so that all escape routes would be cut off. General Crook, with fifteen companies of cavalry and five companies of infantry, moved out from Fort Fetterman, Wyoming, in May 1876. General Terry with 925 men of the Seventh Cavalry and the infantry left Fort Abraham Lincoln in May. Col. John Gibbon led 450 men from a fort near Bozeman, Montana. It was believed that any of the three army units could defeat the Indians. However, unknown to the army officers, thousands of angry Sioux were congregating around Sitting Bull's camp, eager to fight the hated white man.

One engagement between General Crook's troops and the

Sioux was inconclusive, and Crook retreated to his supply base. In a conference aboard the steamboat, the *Far West*, General Terry worked out his strategy based on a scout's report that the Sioux had moved to the Little Bighorn. The plan was for Custer to take the Seventh Cavalry up the Rosebud River until he was above the Indians' presumed location, cross over a ridge connecting the valleys to the Little Bighorn, and then move back downstream. Gibbon would lead his column toward the camp, and, hopefully, the Indians would be caught between them with no chance to escape.

Custer was ambitious and interested in personal glory. If he were to arrive before Gibbon's troops, he could alone take credit for the victory. Custer stripped his men of all but essential gear so that they could move fast and arrive before Gibbon's troops. As Custer and his troops followed the trail of the Indians, he was warned by his scouts that the Indian force was much larger than had been estimated.

On the evening of June 24, Custer approached the part of the trail where he was to move further upstream to ascend the ridge dividing the valley of the Rosebud River from that of the Little Bighorn and then head downstream. Custer decided to disobey his orders and follow the Indians' path into the valley directly to their camp. He was anxious to engage the elusive Indians in battle.

The next day, Custer divided his men into three groups. He and his squadron moved down the bank toward the Little Bighorn. When they finally caught sight of the thousands of Indians in the camp, Custer realized his mistake. He tried to re-gather his troops, but they were no match for the Sioux and were quickly overrun.

More than 270 men including Custer lost their lives at the Battle of Little Bighorn. Indian losses were estimated to be between 40 and 100. By the time Terry's troops arrived on June 27, the Indians had withdrawn and there was a battlefield covered with dead bodies.

Command of the Seventh Cavalry at Fort Lincoln passed to

Col. Samuel Sturgis. During the next six years, the fort continued to protect transportation routes and railroad construction crews as well as government property. When the railroad reached the Montana border, Fort Abraham Lincoln had fulfilled its primary purpose. The Seventh Cavalry headquarters was transferred to Fort Meade in 1882. North Dakota was admitted to statehood in 1889. No longer on the frontier, it had many towns and settlements. Hostile Indians had been subdued and confined to reservations, of which there were only four small ones in North Dakota. The army abandoned Fort Abraham Lincoln in 1891. By 1900, all structures had been dismantled, with materials used in construction of area homes.

In 1907, President Theodore Roosevelt granted 75 acres to the State Historical Society of North Dakota to create Fort Abraham Lincoln State Park. Additional land was acquired until the park reached its present size of 975 acres. In the 1930s the Civilian Conservation Corps rebuilt many of the log and stone structures, infantry blockhouses, and Indian earth lodges.

Tour

Fort Abraham Lincoln State Park is a 975-acre recreational area and historic site. Its scenic location and historic significance contribute to a compelling mystique.

The self-guided tour begins at the **Visitors' Center,** a cut native granite building with flagstone floors and interior trim of native cottonwood. It houses the Fort Lincoln museum, which has extensive exhibits on the Mandan Indians. The Mandan exhibit includes a model of an earth lodge; a diorama of a Mandan village; exhibits on agricultural methods and crops, religious practices, social life, and medicinal plants; and artifacts that include beads, pipes, and tools made of bone.

Another museum exhibit focuses on the Lewis and Clark

Expedition, 1804-06. On October 14, 1804, the explorers camped at On-A-Slant Indian village. There are exhibits on the fur trade and homesteaders.

A military exhibit includes a touch table where you are allowed to handle items including spoons, cartridges, and cups that were discovered during the archeological exploration of the fort. There is a diorama of the fort in 1873, displays of military photographs, and exhibits focusing on the life of frontier soldiers. A slide program on the history of the fort is shown here.

The **Trading Post** is a gift shop selling books and gifts. It is open from 9 A.M. to 5:30 P.M.

The reconstructed **Mandan On-A-Slant Village** is built on the site of the original village as determined by archeological evidence. Only four lodges have been rebuilt—three family earth lodges and a large lodge which was used for religious ceremonies.

Mandan villages were arranged around a central area which held the **Ark of the Lone Man.** According to legend, Lone Man was honored because he was responsible for saving the Mandan nation from a great flood which covered the entire earth. Lone Man constructed a palisade around the Mandan people to protect them from the rising waters. Lone Man's shrine became the focus of the tribe's religious ceremonies. The red post in the center represents the Lone Man and the Mandans. The willow band near the top marks the high stage of the flood.

The **large lodge** or medicine lodge was the site of religious ceremonies. The Mandans believed in many gods but looked up to one superior being who was called the Lord of Life, First Creator, or Great Spirit. Their most elaborate religious ceremony was the O-Kee-Pa, which lasted four days and involved recounting of Mandan legends and asking the Great Spirit for his protection and a good buffalo season; the ceremony also included the induction of young men into manhood, which involved an ordeal of privation and bodily torture. The large lodge was constructed in the same style as the family earth lodges but on a much larger scale.

The three **earth lodges** are circular structures with a log frame covered with grass and mud. Twenty to forty feet in diameter, they were the summer dwellings of an extended family. The sturdy dwellings, cool in summer and warm in the colder months, lasted from eight to ten years and were owned by the women.

Fort Abraham Lincoln consisted of two parts: the infantry post built in 1872 and the cavalry post built in 1873. No original buildings survive since the abandoned buildings were vandalized and dismantled for construction materials by nearby settlers. During the 1930s, the Civilian Conservation Corps conducted archeological surveys to uncover the locations of the military buildings. Interpretative markers are at these locations. The CCC also built the museum/visitor center building and rebuilt some original buildings.

Three **Blockhouses** on the infantry post have been reconstructed. The blockhouses were located at the corners of the palisade which enclosed the post on two sides. The two-story wooden blockhouses have an open area on the top from which the sentry could see in all directions.

There are plans to reconstruct at least five more fort buildings. The only one completed thus far is the **Custer Home.** This large, two-story white house is a reconstruction of the second Custer house as the first one burned down. The second one, built in 1875, contained improvements suggested by the Custers. The imposing house with its large front porch, bay windows, and spacious rooms reflects the status of the post commander.

The outlines of the foundations of other fort buildings are visible, and signs indicate which building it was. Walk the fort areas and read the signs to obtain some idea of the size and variety of fort buildings.

After viewing the historical exhibits, follow the park's

Ridgeline Nature Trail which points out and identifies plant life and geological forms.

Side Trips

The **North Dakota Heritage Center** in Bismarck is an outstanding museum which focuses on North Dakota's history. This modern museum features artistic exhibits on all aspects of North Dakota history from the prehistoric to the contemporary. The State Archives are also located here. There is an excellent book and gift shop. Located on the state capitol grounds in Bismarck, the Heritage Center is open Monday to Thursday from 8 A.M. to 5 P.M., Friday from 8 A.M. to 8 P.M., Saturday from 9 A.M. to 5 P.M., and Sunday from 11 A.M. to 5 P.M. Closed on major holidays. (701) 224-2666.

Fort Totten State Historic Site

Restoration of a mid-nineteenth-century frontier military fort and Indian reservation boarding school, National Register

ADDRESS: P.O. Box 224, Fort Totten, ND 58335
TELEPHONE: (701) 766-4441
LOCATION: In Devils Lake Indian Reservation, 14 miles south of the town of Devils Lake off S.R. 57
OPEN: Daily, mid-May to mid-September, 8 A.M. to 5 P.M.
ADMISSION: Free
FACILITIES: Interpretive Center, film, Little Theater
HOTELS/MOTELS: Trails West Motel, Box 1113, Devils Lake 58301, tel. (701) 662-5011; Super 8 Motel, U.S. 2 East, Devils Lake 58301, tel. (701) 662-8656

CAMPING: K-N-K Campground RV Park, R.R. 1, U.S. 2 West, Devils Lake 58301, tel. (701) 662-7341; Lakewood Park, S.R. 20, Devils Lake 58301; Zebach Camping and Rec. Park, U.S. 2, Devils Lake 58301, tel. (701) 766-4423

History

Fort Totten was established July 17, 1867, on the south side of Devils Lake by Capt. Samuel A. Wainwright. The fort had a twofold mission: to safeguard the emigrants traveling the overland route across Dakota Territory to Montana and to place the Sioux Indians who were in the area on reservations.

The establishment of Devils Lake Indian Reservation for Sisseton, Wahpeton, and Cuthead Sioux was a provision of a treaty signed in February 1867. This Sioux reservation in the Dakota Territory resulted from the 1862 Sioux uprising in Minnesota.

After many Minnesota Sioux moved westward to the buffalo plains in the 1850s, the Santee Sioux who remained became increasingly dissatisfied. The government had managed to acquire all the Indian property for white settlers with the exception of a narrow strip of land, used as a reservation for the Santee Sioux, that was 10 miles wide and 150 miles long on the south side of the Minnesota River.

In payment for their land, these reservation Indians were to receive from the government annuities in goods, food, and cash at two Indian agencies, the Upper and the Lower. The Indians, who had become dependent on these annuities because their hunting lands were gone, became angry and frustrated over delays in issuing their goods. On August 8, 1862, the Santee Sioux went on a rampage, breaking into an Upper Agency storehouse and forcing the distribution of goods.

The uprising caught fire. On August 17, a band of young Sioux from the Lower Agency killed five white people in an apparent show of bravado. Deciding that the whole tribe would probably be punished even if the guilty braves were turned over to white authorities, the tribe from the Lower Agency went on the warpath.

Led by Chief Little Crow, these Sioux viciously attacked and killed white settlers, captured women, and looted and destroyed property. They swept up and down the Minnesota River Valley slaughtering 800 settlers and soldiers. Those who were able to escape took refuge at Fort Ridgely and at New Ulm, a German settlement. The warriors then attacked Fort Ridgely and New Ulm, both of which were able to repel the Indians despite further casualties.

Because of the Civil War, troop strength at frontier forts was very low. However, 1,500 soldiers under the command of Henry Sibley were sent to beleaguered Fort Ridgely, where they arrived August 28. Pursuing the fleeing hostile Indians, Sibley's troops won a decisive victory over Little Crow in the Battle of Wood Lake, Minnesota, on September 23. Two thousand warriors were taken prisoner, but many other hostiles escaped into Dakota Territory.

For the next two years, Santee Sioux, who were joined by Teton Sioux, were relentlessly pursued by Sibley and Brig. Gen. Alfred Sully. The Sioux suffered many losses at the hands of the U.S. troops and eventually disbanded.

Peaceful Sioux, looking for refuge and security, migrated to the Dakota Territory's Devils Lake region, which had a constant water supply, rich vegetation, and abundant wild game and fish. General Sully camped at Devils Lake in July 1865 while still pursuing hostiles. He found a camp of half-breeds and some peaceful, destitute Indians. Sully recommended that a military fort be established at Devils Lake on a reservation for peaceful Indians.

Fort Totten, the military post, was to settle and supervise the Indians with whom the army had so recently been at war. Most Sioux hid from the troops, but gradually the desperate Sioux availed themselves of the protection and provisions of the fort. Since an Indian agent could not be appointed until 500 Indians were at the fort, army rations were shared with the

Indians. By 1870, enough Indians were at the Devils Lake Reservation that William H. Forbes was named Indian agent. As the Indians on the reservation prospered and became farmers, they grew resentful of the placement of Fort Totten Military Reservation, which was within the 360-square-mile Indian reservation and encompassed over one-half of the best land, fresh water, and timber. Although the services of the fort had been essential to the Indian farmers initially, Fort Totten was now viewed as an obstacle to progress. As more and more settlers moved into the Devils Lake region and activity by hostile Indians diminished, the need for a military post also diminished.

On December 21, 1890, the final military unit was withdrawn from Fort Totten. All post buildings and the care of the military reservation were officially turned over to William F. Canfield, the superintendent of the Indian school at Devils Lake Indian Reservation. The military phase of Fort Totten lasted twenty-three years; the remaining sixty-nine years of activity at Fort Totten were as an Indian school.

The boarding school operated at the Devils Lake Indian Reservation was a reflection of a government policy toward Indians during the 1880s. The idea was to civilize and assimilate Indians by educating their young people in boarding schools where influence from tribal culture could be minimized. Some said the idea was to kill the Indian and save the man.

A mission school had been operated by the Grey Nuns at Devils Lake Reservation since 1874. In 1891 the boarding school, open to students aged 7 to 23, commenced.

Believing that the students needed discipline, most Indian boarding schools followed the military-school model which was popular for white youth. They were coeducational. The curriculum was divided between academic subjects—arithmetic, history, English, geography, spelling, and civil government—and industrial training. Boys concentrated on agriculture and livestock production while girls learned the domestic arts.

The first ten years of the boarding school's operation were marred by an unstable budget, harsh discipline, and antagonism from parents who objected to the long separation from their children. Around the turn of the century, students from other reservations were recruited for the underenrolled school. Gradually discipline became more humane, and contact between parents and children was permitted.

A 300-acre farm was operated by the school with all work performed by the students. The farm also supplemented the school's usually inadequate budget. The Fort Totten school originally only went to sixth grade and served about 300 students. In the late 1920s, a high school was added and the curriculum expanded.

Reflecting a new government policy toward Indian education, a day school was added at Fort Totten in 1934. Soon afterward, Fort Totten was changed to a preventorium for the care and education of children with tuberculosis. In 1940, it reverted to a combination day and boarding school. In the late 1950s, the Indian Bureau's policy changed from the assimilation of Indians into the white culture to a belief that Indian progress must be accomplished by the Indians themselves. Therefore, the educational function should be taken over and operated by Indians in their own local schools.

The Fort Totten Indian School closed in 1959 when a new school east of the fort was completed. On March 6, 1959, the fort was transferred from the United States Department of the Interior to the state of North Dakota. Care and maintenance of the fort were assigned to the State Historical Society.

Tour

Fort Totten is a well-preserved, picturesque, historically significant frontier military post. It is one of the finest historic sites in North Dakota and ranks high among forts that have been preserved in the western states. However, to our disappointment, we discovered that the interiors of most buildings have not been restored. The buildings are empty, unfurnished, and locked. This fact greatly diminished our enjoyment, and our hope is that the interiors will be decorated and furnished soon.

Fort Totten's seventeen brick buildings, arranged around a square parade ground, have been well preserved. They are simple one- and two-story rectangular brick structures which were built between 1868 and 1871.

Buildings are either painted white with green trim, denoting the military phase, or gray with maroon trim, denoting the boarding school phase. Apparently when restoration proceeds, some buildings will be returned to their military phase while others will show their school phase. Since most fort buildings were used as both fort and school, most buildings have two signs identifying their usage in each period.

The buildings that are open include the 1868 **Commissary** which is used as an Interpretive Center, small gift shop, and museum with exhibits recounting the history of the fort. Serving as the commissary until the end of the military period, the building was then used as an industrial shop by the school.

The 1869 **Company Quarters**, later **Main School Building**, contains the Fort Totten Little Theater, a summer theater. A pioneer store, stocked with articles typically sold in the nineteenth century, is also in this building.

An orientation film can be viewed at the **Company Quarters—Boys' Dormitory**. An Indian school classroom can also be seen there.

A local history museum called the Lake Region Pioneer Daughters' Museum is located in the 1870 **Hospital and Chapel**, later **Cafeteria**. It is open daily, 1-5 P.M., from Memorial Day through Labor Day.

Buildings that are not open include the **2nd Lieutenant's Quarters—Girls' Sewing Room, Tailor Shop**; the **Captain's and 1st Lieutenants' Quarters—Girls' Dormitory**; the **Commanding Officer's Quarters—Superintendent's Quarters**; the **Captain's and 1st Lieutenants' Quarters—Employees' Quarters and Mess**; the **2nd Lieutenants' Quarters—Chief Clerk's Office**; the **Chaplain's and Surgeon's Quarters—Principal and Married Teachers' Quarters**; the **Magazine—Storage Area**; the **Quartermaster's Storehouse—Bakery, Harness Shop, and Laundry**; the **1930s School Gymnasium**; and the **Adjutant's Office—School Offices**.

6

SOUTH DAKOTA

Prairie Village

Re-creation of a South Dakota rural village of the 1880s-1920s

ADDRESS: Prairie Historical Society, Inc., Box 256, S.R. 34 and U.S. 81, Madison, SD 57042
TELEPHONE: (605) 256-3644
LOCATION: Two miles west of Madison on S.R. 34 and U.S. 81.
OPEN: Daily, 9 A.M. to 6 P.M., from Memorial Day to Labor Day
ADMISSION: Adults, $4; children 6–16, $1.50; group rates available
FACILITIES: Visitors' Center with gift and book shop, picnic area, snack bars, camping

HOTELS/MOTELS: Lake Park Motel, Box 47, U.S. 81, Madison 57042, tel. (605) 256-3524; Pierson Motel, U.S. 81 and S.R. 34, Madison 57042, tel. (605) 256-3536

CAMPING: Prairie Village Campground, Box 256, Madison 57042, tel. (605) 256-3644; Lake Herman State Park, 2 miles west on S.R. 34, Madison 57042, tel. (605) 256-3613

History

South Dakota, one of the Great Plains states, was originally part of a vast expanse of land that was organized as the Iowa Territory by Congress in 1837. What would become the state of South Dakota was the scene of two kinds of economic development. Cattle ranching developed in western South Dakota, which also included the scenic and rugged Black Hills. The eastern and central portions of the soon to be state were settled by homesteaders. These farmer-settlers planted wheat and other crops on what had once been the old buffalo ranges.

To serve the commercial and social needs of the farm families, small towns with schools, community halls, churches, and courthouses were developed. By 1885 the population of South Dakota, now organized as a separate territory, had reached 328,308. In 1889, South Dakota was admitted as a state to the Union. Prairie Village gives the visitor an opportunity to step back in time to the turn of the century to experience life in a small South Dakota town that served the farm families who lived in its vicinity.

Prairie Village is a very active outdoor museum that re-creates South Dakota's rural and small-town heritage. During the summer months, it is the location of fairs, jamborees, horse shows, and other events that attract large crowds to the village. Visitors to these events can immediately feel a sense of small-town hospitality.

This sense of small-town community participation was pre-

sent when the concept of establishing a museum village originated in 1961 at a "threshing bee" held in the area. These
annual threshing bees, organized by the Eastern South Dakota
Threshermen's Association, attracted audiences numbering in
the thousands. Because of the popularity of these events, the
Threshermen's Association reorganized in 1966 as the Prairie
Historical Society, Inc., and decided to develop a permanent
location for the annual threshing exhibition and contest. The
society's decision to preserve South Dakota's history in a setting
that dramatically portrayed its agricultural heritage led to the
development of Prairie Village.

Through the cooperation of many local individuals and
organizations, Prairie Village was created on a 120-acre site,
two miles west of Madison, on the shores of scenic Lake
Herman. Mainly through the work of volunteers, aided by
professional preservationists, the village of sixty buildings was
re-created by moving authentic buildings from South Dakota
to the site and restoring them.

As was true at its origin, the village is the scene of the
Annual Steam Threshing Jamboree which is held during the
last week of August. This event features steam-operated tractors and threshing machines, live entertainment, plowing and
threshing exhibitions and contests, a large flea market, ethnic
foods, and other attractions.

Tour

On your self-guided tour, you will see some of Prairie
Village's most significant buildings.

Note the **Prairie Village Memorial Windmill,** the symbol of
the village. It is a memorial to the region's pioneer settlers.

The **Chapin Lumber Company Building** is the location of
the office, gift shop, and concessions. Visitors should enter the
village here and obtain a map to use on the self-guided tour.

The 1893 **steam carousel,** built by Hirschell Spillman, a

well-known maker of merry-go-rounds, features hand-carved horses from Germany. The carousel is powered by a small steam engine.

The **Antique Car and Tractor Display Barn** and the **Antique Gas and Steam Tractor Display Barn** are large exhibition buildings that house displays of antique automobiles and farm vehicles and equipment. Of special interest are the steam-powered threshing machines and early tractors.

The **log house** was built in 1872 by Lars and Ole Tormsogard, Norwegian immigrants, who homesteaded near Fairview. Its construction reflects the Scandinavian influence and resembles the cabins found in museum villages in Norway and Sweden. It has a well-furnished interior.

The **Sneve Homestead,** the first frame building in Brookings County, was the home of Johannes and Olive Olsen, the parents of Mrs. Svend Sneve. It is a small gray frame house. Its blue, wood-paneled interior contains period pieces such as a table, bed with handmade quilt, and rocking chair.

The **Hyland Country School,** a white frame, one-room school built in the 1880s, was moved from Nunda, where it was designated officially as School No. 11 of the Hyland School District No. 8. Unofficially, it was called the Tobin, Carson, or Tweet school. Country one-room schools, with their locally elected school boards, were institutions of direct democracy and learning in the prairie communities. They offered basic education, largely based on the "three R's" of reading, writing and arithmetic, plus a strong sense of patriotic and moral values, that were reflected in the popular *McGuffey Readers*. The school's light green interior contains a large teacher's desk, both large and small pupils' desks, textbooks, and a piano. It is an excellent example of the small, elementary district, or common school, that was rural America's basic educational institution.

Local ministers conduct services each Sunday during the summer months in the **Junius Methodist Church,** a white frame building erected in 1906 in Junius. Its simply furnished white interior contains a small wooden altar and wooden pews. Like the country school, the church was an important center of community participation.

The **Wentworth Hotel,** a two-story structure built in 1881, was a typical small-town hotel. Its lodgers were usually salesmen who made the rounds of small towns selling goods to local shopkeepers. On the first floor are an entry-reception area, a parlor with a Wing and Son piano and a Brunswick victrola which were used for the entertainment of the guests, a kitchen, and a bedroom. Four additional guest rooms are located upstairs. Its barn, once used to stable the guests' horses, is now used to display tools and small engines.

The **Junius Bank,** a typical small-town financial institution, was built in 1906. It fell victim as did many other small banks to the Wall Street crash of 1929. In its interior are two teller's windows and stations, a manager's desk, and a large vault.

The **Wentworth Railway Depot and Complex** was used originally by the Milwaukee and Burlington Northern (Great Northern) Railway at Wentworth. The Great Northern Railroad was completed under the leadership of financier James J. Hill. Railroads such as the Great Northern hastened the settlement of South Dakota and the other Plains states by bringing settlers to open lands and by carrying agricultural produce to the eastern states and to the world market. At Prairie Village, the railroad complex located near Lake Herman, features two operating steam engines. An unusual feature is the **Chapel Car, "Emmanuel,"** which was used for church services.

The **Battle Creek Telephone Office** houses the telephone exchange which was the communication center for the Wentworth area. A small brown and white frame building, it was the working area of "central," an operator who lived upstairs and worked downstairs at the switchboard.

The **Gross General Store,** built by E.R.C. Gross, is a country store that is stocked with turn-of-the-century merchandise ranging from poultry tonics to high-buttoned shoes. Originally it was the LeRoy Store and Post Office which provided staple groceries and dry goods for area farmers. The general store was an important meeting place for farm families on their weekly trip to town. Gossip was exchanged and purchases were made.

The **Ketcham-Cheatam Coal Company Office** provided fuel for farmers during the long South Dakota winters. The ironic name of the company comes from the last names of the owners who were business partners. Today, the office is a small shop that sells gifts, souvenirs, and books to visitors.

The **dentist office** contains the dental chairs, drills, and equipment of Dr. P. M. Resnvold, one of Madison's early dentists.

The **Hallenbeck-Ellsworth Funeral Home** is located in what was the Madison Hotel, a large two-story frame building. Among exhibits found in museum villages, a funeral parlor is unique. There is a somber display of caskets ranging from a wicker casket to wooden and metal ones. Upstairs are several shops, including a beauty shop, a photography studio, and a dentist's office.

The **Old Madison Hotel,** built in 1878, was moved to Prairie Village in 1975. On the second floor is a toy train collection and a large doll collection.

The **barbershop** was the building used by barber Harold Bitzer. It was moved to Prairie Village from Tolstoy and contains an antique barber chair, razors, and other equipment used by Mr. Bitzer.

The **law office** portrays the office and law library of a small-town attorney. Small-town lawyers were usually occupied in drawing up wills, deeds, and matters involving property rights.

The **Winfred Jail** is a small, frame jail with sturdy two-by-four-foot walls designed to hold offenders. In the interior is an iron prison cage.

The **Ash Grove Seventh-Day Adventist Church,** built in 1882, is a simple, white frame building which originally was located twelve miles north of Madison. It has a plain white interior, dark pews, and altar.

Although it is a new building, the **Electric Museum** was constructed in the 1880's style by the East River Electric Cooperative. Cooperatives, voluntary organizations of consumers, were important in bringing electricity to rural areas. It contains displays of antique electrical items. One area houses an authentic 1890s farm kitchen.

The **First Chartered Library in Dakota Territory,** established in 1886, was located originally in the Howar City Hall. The building was then used exclusively for library purposes. Prairie Village's Chartered Library is unique since libraries of historic vintage are rarely found in museum villages. The Chartered Library has been restored and equipped with a card catalog and book collection. It has historical exhibits on Plains Indians and ethnic groups such as Poles, Norwegians, and Germans who settled in South Dakota.

The **sod house** is a replica of the house occupied by the Jacobs family when they homesteaded in Alberta, Canada, in 1910. Built of prairie sod, such houses were used by homesteaders in certain Plains' regions that were virtually treeless. Its gray plaster interior is well furnished with a bed, table, and other period pieces.

The **claim shanty,** built in 1877 east of Madison, was typical of the type of quickly built shacks which were erected by settlers to establish their land claims. The simply furnished red frame building contains a fur coat, iron bed, chair, and stove.

The **print shop** is a turn-of-the-century weekly newspaper office. The weekly newspaper with its announcements of births, deaths, weddings, and community events was important in reducing the social isolation that often occurred in rural areas. The shop contains printing presses and equipment. Demonstrations of hand-set printing take place during special events at the village.

The **livery barn** was important in rural areas for stabling and outfitting horses in the era prior to the automobile.

The **opera house** was built by the Socialist Party in 1912 in Oldham, where it was used for political meetings, community events, and entertainment. In 1924, Lawrence Welk, a native son of South Dakota, made his stage debut in the hall. It was moved to Prairie Village in 1970 and now serves as the opera house.

The **Junius School,** whose official title was the Winfred School of District No. 4, is a large, white frame building which functioned as a public elementary and high school from 1912–65. The building is now used as an exhibition and demonstration building. It houses an exhibit on the history of Madison's community hospital, which portrays the training of nurses at the hospital during the 1920s. During Jamboree Days, there are demonstrations of quilting and rug weaving.

The **Nicholaison House,** built in 1897 near Rutland, was the homestead of the Johann Nicholaison family. It is furnished with household items owned by the Nicholaisons.

The **George Smith House,** built in 1881, was the home of the Smith family, who were among Lake County's first settlers. The house contains furniture and items owned by the Smith family.

The **gas station** is another structure not commonly found at museum villages. The station was originally located at Iroquois. It portrays the small-town service station with old-style gas pumps.

Among the other buildings that can be visited at Prairie Village are the **farm blacksmith shop,** an old **carpenter shop,** the **Chautauqua Ticket Office,** and a **bandstand.**

Side Trips

The **Siouxland Heritage Museums,** a joint city-county museum system, located in Sioux Falls, consists of the **Old Courthouse Museum** and the **Pettigrew Home and Museum.** The Old Courthouse Museum, downtown at Sixth and Main, was designed by architect Wallace Dow. An excellent example of the Richardsonian-Romanesque style of architecture, it served as the county courthouse until 1962 when it became a museum. While Gallery I features changing exhibits, Gallery II houses permanent exhibits on the settlement of the Siouxland area by different ethnic groups. It also contains exhibits illustrating the development of the "Great American Desert" into a productive agricultural and commercial region.

The **Pettigrew Home** was built in 1889 for the T.B. McMartin family. From 1911–26, it was the residence of Richard F. Pettigrew, South Dakota's first United States senator. The home now serves as a museum for Pettigrew's natural history specimens and his collection of American Indian artifacts. Information about both museums can be obtained from the Siouxland Heritage Museums, 200 W. Sixth St., Sioux Falls, SD 57102; tel. (605) 335-4210.

The Old Courthouse and the Pettigrew Home are open Tuesday through Saturday from 9 A.M. to 5 P.M. and on Sunday and Monday from 1 P.M. to 5 P.M. Closed major holidays. Admission is free.

The **Friends of the Middle Border Museum of Pioneer Life,** 1311 S. Duff St., Mitchell, SD 57301-7071, tel. (605) 996-2122, is a museum village complex that includes a restored 1886 home, the Dakota art gallery, a territorial school, general store, and other exhibits. Open June–August, from 8 A.M. to 6 P.M.,, Monday–Saturday, and from 10 A.M. to 6 P.M., Sunday. Open May and September, from 9 A.M. to 5 P.M., Monday–Friday, and from 1–5 P.M., Saturday and Sunday. Open October–April, 9 A.M. to 5 P.M., Monday–Friday. Admission for adults is $2; senior citizens, $1.50; students 12 and over, $1.

PART II

LOWER GREAT PLAINS

7

ARKANSAS

Arkansas Territorial Restoration

Restoration of Little Rock village during Arkansas's territorial-to-statehood period, late 1820s to 1850

ADDRESS: Third and Scott Streets, Little Rock, AR 77201
TELEPHONE: (501) 371-2348
LOCATION: Downtown Little Rock
OPEN: Daily, Monday–Saturday, 9 A.M. to 5 P.M.; Sunday, 1 to 5 P.M. Closed Christmas Eve, Christmas Day, New Year's Day, Easter, and Thanksgiving.
ADMISSION: Adults, $1; children and senior citizens, 25 cents
FACILITIES: Visitors' Center with art gallery, native craft store, and slide show
HOTELS/MOTELS: Holiday Inn—City Center, 617 S. Broadway,

Little Rock 72201, tel. (501) 376-2071; Hilton Inn Riverfront, 2 Riverfront Pl., Little Rock 72114, tel. (501) 371-9000; Capital Hotel, 111 W. Markham St., Little Rock 72201, tel. (501) 374-7474.

CAMPING: Moro Bay State Park, Star Route, Jersey 71651, tel. (501) 463-8555; Maumeller, Murray Lock and Dam, Overlook Dr., Little Rock 72207, tel. (501) 329-2986; Gulpha Gorge, Hot Springs National Park, P.O. Box 1860, Hot Springs 71902, tel. (501) 624-3383; KOA Benton, S.R. 7, Box 1440, Benton 72015, tel. (501) 778-1244.

History

Arkansas was a part of the Louisiana Purchase and was originally administered through the Missouri Territory. In 1819, Arkansas became a separate territory under President James Monroe. People who migrated to the new territory settled along the rivers and along the Southwest Trail which crossed Arkansas from the northeast to the southwest.

The first territorial capital was at Arkansas Post, Arkansas's first white settlement established in 1684 by Henri de Tonti. Only ten years after Arkansas became a territory, the capital was moved to Little Rock, which was at the geographic center of the territory. Located on the Arkansas River, the Little Rock area represents a natural dividing line between the region's hill country and flatlands.

Early Arkansas River travelers took their bearing from Big Rock, a bare stone face north of the river. Two miles downstream, on the other bank, was a smaller rock outcropping which became known as Little Rock. It was from this landmark that the capital city got its name.

River traffic moved people and goods to and from the town. The population at Little Rock grew from 1,500 residents in 1840 to 3,700 in 1860; 13,000 in 1880; and 38,000 in 1900. By 1860 the town contained many large buildings, a federal arsenal, a college, a female seminary, and three newspapers. The *Arkansas Gazette*, published by William Woodruff, is still in circulation today. Woodruff was indentured as an apprentice to a New York printer, Alden Spaner, in 1810. Spaner set Woodruff free in 1818 and he traveled to Arkansas. In 1819, Woodruff founded the *Arkansas Gazette* at Arkansas Post. When the capital was moved to Little Rock, Woodruff followed.

As Little Rock expanded and modernized in the twentieth century, original frontier buildings near the Arkansas River fell into disrepair. The downtown's commercial and business area expanded into the old residential area.

Restoration of the city's early nineteenth-century structures began in 1939 spurred on by a campaign led by Louise Loughborough, a descendant of William Fulton, Arkansas's last territorial governor. The Works Progress Administration began working on the historic buildings in 1939, and the Arkansas Territorial Restoration was opened in July 1941. It is operated by the Department of Arkansas Heritage.

Tour

The Arkansas Territorial Restoration is one square block in the downtown area of the capital city. Entering through a modern **Visitors' Center,** start your tour by watching the slide program which emphasizes Arkansas's involvement in the western frontier. A tour guide takes you through each museum building.

Once you leave the contemporary Visitors' Center, the setting is mid-nineteenth-century Little Rock. Red brick and white frame houses are interspersed with flower and herb gardens and red brick paths. Huge magnolia and elm trees provide plenty of shade.

The **Hinderliter kitchen** is a separate, small white frame

outbuilding where cooking was done for the Hinderliter House
and Grog Shop. Rebuilt in 1939, the kitchen has a brick floor,
a large, almost walk-in, brick fireplace, and white plank walls.
Pottery and china are stored in a jelly cupboard and a pie safe.
Many long-handled iron and copper utensils and iron pots are
clustered around the fireplace.

The **Hinderliter Grog Shop or Tavern,** built in the 1820s, is
the oldest extant building in Little Rock and is believed to be
the only frame building remaining from Arkansas's territorial
period. The large, two-story house was originally constructed
of logs. Subsequently, the oak logs were covered with hand-
beaded, red-heart cypress siding. The house was owned by
Jesse Hinderliter, who operated a grog shop on the first floor
and had living quarters upstairs.

The Grog Shop is a large room on the first floor complete
with cage bar. Furnishings include tables and chairs for card-
playing. The wooden floors are painted red while the wooden
walls are white. The attractive tavern has a fireplace and a
beam ceiling.

The family dining room has a hand-carved, Federal-style
fireplace, green walls, and dark red painted floor. In the
hallway, which has both a front and back entrance, stand
trunks belonging to travelers who stayed in the upstairs rooms.
One of the upstairs bedrooms has had the wallboards removed
to display the original log construction. Bedrooms are furnished with rope beds, and the master bedroom has a mammy
bench. One room served as an artist's studio.

The **Brownlee/Noland House,** built in the 1840s, is a red
brick, Federal-style house with green shutters. It was built by a
Scottish stonemason named Robert Brownlee for his brother
James. A territorial legislator and author named C.F.M.
Noland lived in the house in the 1850s, and many of his
possessions are displayed. The well-decorated house has a
center entry with a bedroom with a sleigh bed to the right and
a parlor with a hand-carved mantel painted like marble to the
left. Windows have wooden venetian blinds.

The **McVicar-Conway House** was moved to this site from a nearby location. The small frame house was built in the 1840s for James McVicar, who combined careers as a stonemason and a warden of the state penitentiary. Later, the house was owned by the Conway family, who were politically prominent during the frontier period. This southern-style home has a small entranceway with both front and back doors. The bedroom is on one side while the parlor with Conway's desk and chair is on the other. A breezeway connects the parlor to the kitchen, which has a fireplace for cooking. A large kitchen cabinet has original glass in its doors. Outside the kitchen is a well which was added in 1939 when the house was moved.

The **Woodruff Exhibit** consists of the buildings used by William Woodruff as his home and his printing office after the *Arkansas Gazette* was moved to Little Rock in 1824. The print shop is in a small, two-room building. It contains a printing press, boxes of type, Woodruff's desk, tables, and chairs, and an 1838 map of Arkansas. The Woodruff kitchen has an exhibit on Woodruff's journey to Arkansas Post from Fireplace, New York.

Another building in the Woodruff Exhibit has a time-line exhibit on important historical events in both Arkansas and the country from 1819–61. Articles from the *Arkansas Gazette* illustrate each event, making a fascinating exhibit. A medicinal herb garden is outside the house.

The **Plum Bayou Log House** is a pre-Civil War log house with a dog trot. It is used as a hands-on educational center for grade school children. Costumed interpreters assist children in frontier activities like spinning, weaving, dyeing, and candlemaking. The building is not open for viewing by the general public.

Two special events held at the Arkansas Territorial Restoration are the Craft Show and Festival in May, which features Arkansas crafts, music, food, and entertainment, and the Christmas Open House in December.

Side Trips

Hot Springs National Park, with its 47 hot springs, became a popular bathing and health spa in an earlier era. As early as 1832, the federal government reserved the springs for public use. Although the park encompasses 5,827 acres, most of that acreage is outside the city of Hot Springs. The springs which belong to the national park are in the resort city of Hot Springs. The arrangement worked out was that the government controlled the spring water and supplied it to the bathhouses, which were privately owned.

Although bathing spas are no longer fashionable, the town of Hot Springs is still a busy resort center. There are elegant old resort hotels. Bathhouse Row is lined with ornate bathhouses, some of which can be toured and baths still can be taken. The area has a moderate climate, and the park has an 18-mile network of wooded hiking trails in the Zig Zag mountains outside the town. Camping is available at Gulpha Gorge, and there are picnic areas and a visitors' center. The address is P.O. Box 1860, Hot Springs, AR 71902; tel. (501) 624-3383.

Traditional resort hotels are the Arlington Resort Hotel and Spa, Central Ave. at Fountain St., Hot Springs 71901, tel. (501) 623-7771 or (800) 643-1502; and the Majestic Resort-Spa, Park and Central Ave., Hot Springs 71901, tel. (501) 623-5511 or (800) 643-1504.

Old Washington Historic State Park

Restoration and reconstruction of southwestern Arkansas town during territorial and early statehood periods, 1824–74; National Register

ADDRESS: P.O. Box 98, Washington, AR 71862
TELEPHONE: (501) 093-2684 or (501) 983-2898
LOCATION: On S.R. 4, 9 miles northwest of Hope and 18 miles southeast of Nashville; from I-30, Exit 30, 8 miles north on S.R. 4
OPEN: 9 A.M. to 4 P.M., Monday and Wednesday–Saturday; 1 to 5 P.M., Sunday; closed Tuesday, Thanksgiving, Easter, Christmas Eve, Christmas Day, and New Year's Day
ADMISSION: Adults, $3; children 6–15, $1; group rates available
FACILITIES: Visitors' Center, gift shop, Williams Tavern Restaurant open for breakfast and lunch; Southwest Arkansas Regional Archives
MOTELS: Best Western Tradewinds Inn, northwest corner of junction I-30 and S.R. 4, Hope 71801, tel. (501) 777-6755; Holiday Inn, I-30 and S.R. 4, Hope 71801, tel. (501) 777-8601
INNS: Old County Jail, P.O. Box 157, Washington 71862, tel. (501) 983-2178
CAMPING: Crater of Diamonds State Park, Rt. 1, Box 364, Murfreesboro, tel. (501) 285-3113; Daisy State Park, Daisy Route, Box 66, Kirby 71950, tel. (501) 398-4487; White Oak Lake State Park, Star Route, Bluff City 71722, tel. (501) 685-2748

History

The town of Washington, located near the Red River on a hill where four Indian trails crossed the Southwest Trail, was founded in 1824. This little corner of Arkansas was a part of the Louisiana Territory which in 1682 was claimed for France by the explorer La Salle. In 1762 the Treaty of Paris, which ended the French-Indian War, ceded the Louisiana Territory to Spain. In 1803, France resumed ownership for a few weeks, just long enough to sell the land to the United States for $15 million.

After becoming United States property, what is now the

state of Arkansas was governed as a part of the New Madrid District of the Louisiana Territory until 1806, when the larger part became the Arkansas District. In 1812, after Louisiana became a state, the Arkansas District was attached to the Territory of Missouri. In 1819 the Territory of Arkansas was created from the southern half of the Missouri Territory.

When the Louisiana Purchase was opened to settlement, homesteaders streamed into the Arkansas Territory. The population jumped from 14,273 in 1820 to more than 50,000 in 1835. Soon there was pressure for statehood; Arkansas became a state in June 1836.

Many settlers traveled on the Southwest Trail, which passed through Washington. The Southwest Trail ran from the Mississippi River across a corner of present-day Missouri, then went southwest across Arkansas for almost three hundred miles to the Red River. The origins of the Southwest Trail are unknown; it could have begun as an Indian buffalo hunter's trail. The Spanish called it the Chihuahua Trail.

In 1819, the year Arkansas became a territory, Rev. William Stevenson, a Methodist preacher, built a huge log shed on the side of the hill by the Black Bois d'Arc Creek for Methodist revival camp meetings. He called it "The Ebenezer Campground." Soon the town of Washington grew up around the campground. Elijah Stuart built a tavern on the rise of the hill. Nearby, William Shaw built a blacksmith shop.

In 1824 the U.S. Congress granted three-quarters of a section of land to all counties in the Arkansas Territory for the location of a permanent seat of justice. The commissioners of the county of Hempstead, one of whom was Elijah Stuart, decided to locate Hempstead County's permanent seat of justice at the head of the Black Bois d'Arc Creek. The Court of Common Pleas for Hempstead County was held in Elijah Stuart's tavern until 1825, when the hewn log Hempstead Courthouse was built on the crown of the hill.

As white settlers moved into the vast lands acquired from France, they encroached on the hunting and tribal lands of the

Indians. Siding with the whites' right to these lands, the United States established an official policy of relocating eastern Indian tribes across the Mississippi River. Some Indians agreed to the move, but many, especially the Cherokee, refused. The Removal Bill of 1830 provided for the forceable removal of the Indians. Some of the forced marches to the west, referred to as the "Trail of Tears," were on the Southwest Trail which ran through Washington. Money appropriated by Congress to improve this trail was in anticipation of the Indian removal. Some Washington businessmen obtained government contracts to sell food to the Choctaw and Chickasaw Indians who marched through the town.

Washington's other tangential claims to fame include having one of the town's blacksmiths, James Black, make the first Bowie knife—maybe. As the story is told in Washington, Jim Bowie brought a design of a knife whittled out of a cigar box cover to James Black and asked him to make it. Black made two knives, one according to Bowie's design and one of his own design. Bowie bought Black's design, and Bowie's name became associated with the famous knife. There are other stories about the origin of the Bowie knife.

Another Washington story involves Sam Houston, who is said to have spent time at the Washington tavern while making plans for the liberation of Texas. He is said to have met with Stephen Austin and Jim Bowie in Washington also. Because of Washington's proximity to the Texas border, it was a natural stopping-off place before entering Mexican-held Texas. Davy Crockett and his men stayed in Washington for several days in November 1835 before joining Houston's army in Texas.

During the Mexican-American War, which started in 1846, Washington was designated as the rendezvous point for volunteers to be enrolled and mustered into service. The first volunteer soldiers arrived in late June, and more soldiers kept coming all during the summer and fall. Men on their way to fight in Mexico were encamped in and around Washington. When the war ended in the fall of 1847, the columns of cavalry and infantry and artillery came marching up the Southwest Trail, through Washington, and back to their homes.

Washington's greatest prominence derives from it being the Confederate state capital of Arkansas from 1863–65 during the Civil War. Arkansas joined the southern states that seceded from the Union. Many slaves were used on the large cotton plantations in the Washington area. Washington young men marched off to war.

In September 1863, Gen. Frederick Steele captured Little Rock, the capital of Arkansas. Residents of Little Rock fled the city and moved into the only part of the state still held by the Confederates—the southwestern part. Every attic and basement of every house in Washington held women and children who had fled before the Union army. Some companies of the Confederate army had also moved southwest, and the fields near Washington were filled with soldiers and army tents. Confederate generals set up headquarters in the area.

Governor Harris Flanagan of Arkansas moved to Washington, as did the state government. Setting up headquarters in the Hempstead Courthouse, the general assembly and the supreme court continued to function. Even the state archives had been moved to Washington. Washington became the center of state Confederate activities, and its town newspaper, *The Washington Telegraph*, was the only rebel newspaper still publishing in the state.

Meanwhile in federally held Little Rock, General Steele had set up a federal government with Isaac Murphy as governor; thus, there were two state governments in Arkansas. General Steele even requested that the state archives be returned to Little Rock, but Governor Flanagan did not comply.

In the spring, Gen. Frederick Steele and Gen. N.P. Banks attempted a pincers movement to trap the Confederate armies in southern Arkansas and northern Louisiana. Banks moved up the Red River toward Shreveport, while Steele marched southwest from Little Rock and occupied Camden. Banks was repulsed in Louisiana, and Steele retreated to Little Rock because Confederate detachments were capturing his supply trains and the spring rains made the roads nearly impassable.

After the war ended, the townspeople began rebuilding their lives again. Reconstruction was tolerable, but Washington was dealt a severe blow when the Cairo and Fulton Railroad came to southwest Arkansas in 1874, bypassing Washington by eight miles to run through the new town of Hope. When fire swept through Washington in 1874, burning many businesses, many business people decided to rebuild in Hope. After the fire of 1883, in which twenty-four businesses burned, the same phenomenan occurred. Washington's highest population of 780 people in 1880 began falling.

The move for restoration of the town began in 1958 with local citizens founding the Community Improvement Club and the Foundation for the Restoration of Pioneer Washington. In 1973 the Arkansas State Parks and Tourism Department was brought in as a partner and Washington became the Old Washington Historic State Park.

Tour

Old Washington Historic State Park preserves a collection of restored buildings in the small town of Washington. Because it was bypassed by the railroad, the town did not prosper and grow. It retains a mid-nineteenth-century air with quiet streets, huge magnolia trees, spacious lawns, and lovely gardens. Our early spring visit coincided with hundreds of daffodils in bloom. The peacefulness of the town contributes to the sense of being in a time warp. The restored buildings are interspersed with privately owned and occupied residences.

Purchase your tour tickets and get your map for a self-guided tour at the **Hempstead County Courthouse,** which serves as the Visitors' Center. There is also a gift shop and the

Southwest Arkansas Regional Archives. The red brick, two-story Victorian building has the year it was built, 1874, in black iron numerals over the door. This third Washington courthouse was used from 1874 until 1939, when Hope became the county seat.

The **Williams Tavern Restaurant,** which can be visited without a tour ticket, serves breakfast and lunch in its restored dining rooms. The entry has a cage bar while the dining rooms have wooden plank floors, beamed ceilings, and fireplaces. Waitresses wear period costumes, and the menu has traditional dishes. The vegetarian plate came with baked beans, baked corn, and dill flavored turnip greens. The coconut custard pie was very much like a pecan pie. The tavern was built by John W. Williams in 1832 at Marlbrook, seven miles northeast, and moved to the Washington site.

The **Tavern Inn** is a reconstruction of the original tavern built by Joshua Morrison in the 1830s. The two-story, white frame building has wide verandas on both the first and second floors. The first-floor taproom is a large, bright room with a wooden bar, a fireplace, tables and chairs for card-playing, an 1850 reed organ, and a piano. The inn's detached kitchen is an outstanding feature in terms of both size and decor. Detached because of the possible fire hazard to the inn, the large kitchen has cathedral ceilings, a huge brick fireplace, a large table, a pie safe, and a collection of flow blue and willow blue china. At one end of the room is a loom, spinning wheel, and oversized baskets of cotton.

The **Blacksmith Shop,** on Conway Street, is a log reconstruction of the shop where James Black is said to have made the first Bowie knife. It is a working blacksmith shop with demonstrations by a guide who also retells the Bowie legend.

The most important historic site in Washington is the white frame **Courthouse,** which was built in 1836 and was used as the Confederate state capital from 1863–65. The first floor, which was formerly divided into rooms, is now one large room. Its floors, ceilings, panelled walls, and hand-hewn columns of yellow pine are original. Two fireplaces stand at opposite ends of the room. The walls are adorned with portraits of Robert E. Lee, Stonewall Jackson, Bradley Johnson, and General Beauregard. Among the Civil War artifacts displayed are Confederate and state money. The courtroom was on the second floor, which is now used for Masonic meetings.

The **B.W. Edwards Weapons Museum,** housed in a former bank building, contains the guns collected by Edwards. Among the hundreds of foreign and American weapons are rifles, pistols, revolvers, swords, Remingtons, flintlocks, and Bowie knifes.

The **Sanders House** was built in Greek Revival style in 1845 by Simon T. Sanders. One of Sanders' daughters, Sarah Virginia, married Augustus H. Garland, who became the governor of Arkansas, U.S. senator, and Attorney General under President Cleveland. The house has fifteen-foot ceilings and the original cypress floors. Due to a somewhat unusual floor plan, some bedrooms and the dining room may only be entered from the outside porch.

The **Purdon House,** built arond 1850, holds medical exhibits relating to the practice of medicine in Washington.

The **Royston Log House,** which was built around 1835, was moved to Washington from the Royston Plantation in 1986. It is a two-room house built of logs that have been covered by planks. The kitchen has a front and back door, and a double-sided fireplace serves both kitchen and bedroom.

The **Royston House** is another Greek Revival house with Empire furniture.

Side Trips

White Oak Lake State Park, situated among the wooded rolling hills of south-central Arkansas, has the second largest lake in Arkansas. With facilities for camping, picnicking, swimming, fishing, and boating, it is located on S.R. 387, south of Bluff City. The address is Star Route, Bluff City, AR 71722; tel. (501) 685-2748.

Crater of Diamonds State Park has 888 pine-covered acres along the banks of the Little Missouri River. Its unique attraction is the 40-acre field where diamonds can be found. It is the only diamond area in North America open to the public. Other semiprecious gems, including amethyst and agate, and minerals can also be found. Camping, picnicking, and hiking are available. It is located two miles southeast of Murfreesboro on S.R. 301. The address is Rt. 1, Box 364, Murfreesboro, AR 71958; tel. (501) 285-3113.

Prairie Grove Battlefield State Park

Civil war battlefield and re-creation of an Arkansas Civil War era town; National Register

ADDRESS: P.O. Box 306, Prairie Grove, AR 72753
TELEPHONE: (501) 846-2990
LOCATION: From U.S. 71 Bypass in Fayetteville, west on U.S. 62 just 8 miles to the park
OPEN: Daily, 8 A.M. to 5 P.M.; closed Thanksgiving, Christmas Eve, Christmas Day, New Year's Day; guided tours hourly from 9 A.M. to 4 P.M., Memorial Day through Labor Day and by request during rest of the year
ADMISSION: Free
FACILITIES: Visitors' Information Center with gift shop and audiovisual slide orientation; picnic areas with tables, grills, barbeque pits; playground, restrooms, and pavillion
HOTELS/MOTELS: Best Western Inn, 1000 U.S. 71 Bypass,

Stores, Amana, Amana Colonies, Iowa

1867 Barn, Flynn Farmstead, Living History Farms, Des Moines, Iowa

1820 Commandant's House and Barracks, Historic Fort Snelling, St. Paul, Minnesota

Nebraska Midland Railroad Engine and Coal Car, Stuhr Museum of the Prairie Pioneer, Grand Island, Nebraska

1869 Elm Creek Fort, Warp's Pioneer Village, Minden, Nebraska

Reconstructed Adjutant's Office and Guardhouse where Crazy Horse died, Fort Robinson State Park, Crawford, Nebraska

Telephone Museum and 1920 Drug Store, Bonanzaville USA-Pioneer Village and Museum, West Fargo, North Dakota

1895 Dobrinz School, Bonanzaville USA-Pioneer Village and Museum, West Fargo, North Dakota

Reconstructed Mandan Earthlodges, On-A-Slant Village, Fort Abraham Lincoln State Park, Mandan, North Dakota

Company Quarters – 1869 Boys' Dormitory, Fort Totten State Historic Site, Devil's Lake, North Dakota

Gas Station from Iroquois, South Dakota, Prairie Village, Madison, South Dakota

1820 Hinderliter Grog Shop and Summer Kitchen, Arkansas Territorial Restoration, Little Rock, Arkansas

1836 Confederate State Capitol, Old Washington Historic State Park, Washington, Arkansas

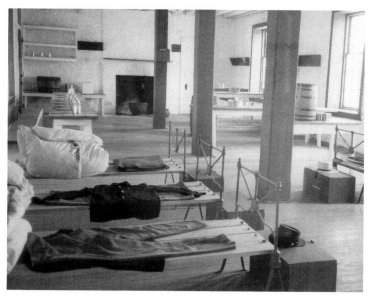

1845 Barracks Interior, Fort Gibson, Fort Gibson, Oklahoma

Columns remaining from Cherokee Female Seminary, Cherokee National Museum, Tsa-La-Gi, Tahlequah, Oklahoma

Fayetteville 72701, tel. (501) 442-3041; Ramada Inn, 3901 N. College Ave., Fayetteville 72701, tel. (501) 443-3431; Mountain Inn, 21 S. College Ave., Fayetteville 72701, tel. (501) 521-1000

CAMPING: Devil's Den State Park, West Fork 72774, tel. (501) 761-3325; Lake Weddington, Ozark National Forest, P.O. Box 1008, Russellville 72801, tel. (501) 667-2191; Beaver Lake, Drawer H, Rogers 72756, tel. (501) 636-1210

History

Travelers to historic sites have two reasons to visit Prairie Grove Battlefield State Park. Those interested in Civil War history can walk the lines where more than 18,000 Union and Confederate troops clashed on December 7, 1862. Second, an Ozark village, typical of northwest Arkansas, has been recreated by moving authentic buildings to the park.

Arkansas, as both a territory and a state, occupied a strategic location in American history. In the 1830s it was a point of departure for Americans who were moving into Texas. Those who plotted to secure Texas independence from Mexico met on Arkansas territory to plan their strategies. During the Civil War, Arkansas was again a strategic area for both control of the Mississippi River Valley and for movement to Texas and the Southwest.

After the election of Abraham Lincoln as president, Arkansas seceded and joined ten other southern states to form the Confederacy. In 1861, northwestern Arkansas was a key area in the Confederate strategy to win independence. It was a rich agricultural area, a source of manpower, and the point of entry to the Indian Territory, now Oklahoma, and Texas.

War came to Arkansas in late February 1862 when a 10,500-man Union army commanded by Maj. Gen. Samuel R. Curtis invaded the state by way of neighboring Missouri.

The Union force was met by a Confederate army of 16,000 men led by Maj. Gen. Earl Van Dorn. In the battle of Pea Ridge, the Confederates were defeated and retreated farther south and west into Arkansas. The Confederates were further weakened by the diversion of troops to fight at Shiloh in Tennessee and Vicksburg in Mississippi.

Jefferson Davis, Confederate president, named Gen. Thomas Carmichael Hindman, a former Arkansas congressman, to command the beleaguered southern forces on May 26, 1862. Hindman energetically reorganized the Confederate defenses, claiming that he would "drive out the invader or perish." Successful in reinvigorating the Confederate forces, Hindman prepared to invade Missouri. Responding to Hindman's threat, the federal troops were reorganized as the Army of the Frontier. The stage was now set for the battle of Prairie Grove on December 7, 1862. It was here that Hindman sought to defeat the Union army of Brig. Gens. James G. Blunt and Francis J. Herron and regain control of northwest Arkansas for the Confederacy.

Prairie Grove, the site where the opposing armies clashed, was a large ten-square-mile prairie. Hindman chose to deploy his 11,000 Confederate troops along a one-and-a-half-mile battleline running along a ridge, with wooded ravines, straddling the Fayetteville-Cane Hill Road and covering the main crossing over the Illinois River. The battle began with Confederate cavalry in pursuit of a Union cavalry force which was an advance unit of Union Gen. Francis Herron's two divisions, numbering 8,500 men.

A division of the Union army was held in reserve at Cane Hill, six miles southwest, commanded by Gen. James G. Blunt. The main battle ensued for two days, December 7 and 8, with the Confederates determined to hold the long ridge, repel the invaders, and chase the Union forces back across the Arkansas border into Missouri. After initial artillery duels and a series of inconclusive infantry charges, the Confederates were forced to withdraw because of the depletion of their stores of ammunition and the arrival of Union reserves at a crucial stage in the battle.

The combined casualties of both sides were 2,500 dead, wounded, and missing. Hindman's Confederates withdrew and the Union was in control of northwest Arkansas, the gateway to both the southern part of the state and the Indian Territory (Oklahoma). Visitors can take a walking tour of the battlefield, which is described in the tour.

In addition to the battlefield, the park has a small northwest Arkansas Ozark village which is composed of authentic structures that have been moved to the site and restored. Northwest Arkansas was settled by people who came to the territory by way of the Mississippi River or across country from Tennessee. The first settlers to the area were log cabin dwellers. Lack of good roads, impassable swamps, and an underdeveloped transportation system produced small farms and frontier communities that were isolated from each other. A typical rural Ozark mountain community has been re-created in the park. The backwoods song, "Arkansas Traveler," by Col. Sandy Falkner, recounts the lack of sophistication and isolation associated with the Arkansas Territory, which was established in 1819. The new territory contained a mixture of hunters, squatters, small farmers, land speculators, and plantation owners. The Ozark Mountains and the hill country saw a folk culture emerge that resembled that of the mountainous areas of Virginia, North Carolina, and Tennessee. On June 15, 1836, Arkansas was admitted as a state. Populated by people with southern sympathies, Arkansas seceded from the Union to join the Confederacy.

Tour

The battlefield can be toured by a ten-mile self-guided driving or walking tour. Only 130 acres of the 3,200-acre battleground are located in the state park. The complete tour requires traveling over some state and country roads located outside the park. The tour should begin at the Battlefield Museum, where park staff can supply maps and information. The **Battlefield Museum and Visitors' Center,** built as a memorial to Confederate Gen. Thomas C. Hindman, contains a diorama and artifacts of the battle of Prairie Grove. Visitors should view the audiovisual orientation program for an overview of the battle and the park. The museum provides displays of military uniforms, firearms, shells, and artillery pieces used by both Confederate and Union forces. Documents, letters, and photographs relating to the participants in the battle are also exhibited.

Tour Stop 1 identifies the ridge where Confederate Brigadier General Shoup, with the approval of his commander, General Hindman, established the Confederate battle positions.

Tour Stop 2 locates the Borden house sector, the scene of some of the heaviest fighting. During the battle, the house was alternately occupied by Confederate and then Union soldiers who used its upper story as a location for snipers.

Tour Stop 3 marks the location of the Confederate right flank commanded by Col. Emmett MacDonald's Missouri (C.S.A.) cavalry.

Tour Stop 4 is the location of the Borden wheatfield where Lt. Joseph Foust's Missouri artillery battery (Union) was positioned.

Tour Stop 5 is the main Fayetteville-Cane Hill Road crossing of the Illinois River, where several diversionary actions occurred.

Tour Stop 6 marks the location where the Thompson house once stood. Here, Herron's Union division took up its position, and his artillery inflicted heavy damage on the Confederate positions on the ridge.

Tour Stop 7, the Borden cornfield, marks the scene of some of the battle's heaviest infantry actions. Advancing Union infantry were repulsed by Hindman's troops. The pursuing Confederates suffered heavy casualties when they reached the

Union lines where artillery fired canisters at them at short ranges.

Tour Stop 8 was the location of the Ada Post Office, one of the few buildings on the battlefield.

Tour Stop 9 was the location of the Hugh Rogers' house which was used by Confederate snipers. The house was destroyed in the battle.

Tour Stop 10 identifies the positions of a Confederate brigade commanded by Brig. Gen. M. Monroe Parson.

Tour Stop 11, the Morton hayfield, was the scene of an advance by Union troops of the First Indian Home Guard, primarily Creeks and Cherokees, from the Indian Territory.

Tour Stop 12, the Morton house sector, marks the scene where Union troops, commanded by Blunt, advanced but encountered concentrated opposition from Confederate forces. Unable to continue their advance, Blunt's forces retired to the base of the ridge. The house no longer stands, and the area today is occupied by the Prairie Grove schools.

Tour Stop 13 locates Wilson's field where Lt. Marcus Tenney's Kansas battery, supported by Illinois, Wisconsin, and Missouri cavalry units, gave fire support to Blunt's infantry.

Tour Stop 14, the road to Rhea's mill, is where Blunt joined his forces with Herron's right flank.

Tour Stop 15 designates where the left flank of Frost's Confederate division rested. Located nearby were Texas cavalry units.

Tour Stop 16 marks the location of the Prairie Grove church which was used by Hindman of the Confederate forces. The battlefield and the park are named for the church.

The re-created Ozark Village can be visited by guided tour. Among the restored buildings that have been moved to the site are:

The **Morrow House,** moved to Prairie Grove from Cove Creek, was used as the headquarters of General Hindman, the Confederate commander, during the battle. It also served as a field hospital for wounded soldiers. It now features exhibits on the background of the Morrow family, the impact of the Civil War on Ozark culture, and exhibits on society, culture, education, religion, agriculture, and commerce in northwestern Arkansas. The living room, furnished in nineteenth-century Ozark fashion, contains a bed, wardrobe, table, and other period items.

The **Latta House** was built in 1834 by John Latta, who called his Ozark home "The Lord's Vineyard." Moved from Evansville, its spacious white living room on the first floor is furnished with a large table and chairs, spinning wheel, and rocking chairs. The second floor contains two bedrooms furnished with period pieces. Other buildings that are part of the Latta House complex are a large barn, a well house, a detached kitchen, and a smokehouse.

The **Village Church,** dating from the 1880s, and the **Village School,** dating from 1894, represent buildings that were commonly part of small Ozark mountain settlements. Other representative structures found in the park are the **blacksmith shop,** the **sorghum mill,** a **dogtrot cabin,** and a **general store.**

While not in the restored Ozark village, the **Bordon House,** used by Confederate snipers during the battle, is still another historic structure that is located in the park.

Side Trips

Pea Ridge National Military Park, Pea Ridge, AR 72751, tel. (501) 451-8122, located 43 miles from Prairie Grove, marks the location of the largest battle of the Civil War fought west of the Mississippi River. The park's Visitors' Center is located 10 miles north of Rogers off U.S. 62. The park commemorates the battle of Pea Ridge, fought on March 7–8, 1862, between Confederate and Union armies. The Union victory gave the federal government complete control of Missouri. It is open daily from 8 A.M. to 5 P.M., except for December 25 and January 1, when the park is closed.

8

OKLAHOMA

Fort Gibson Military Park

Restoration of a U.S. Military Fort, 1824–90; National Register, National Historic Landmark

ADDRESS: P.O. Box 457, Fort Gibson, OK 74434
TELEPHONE: (918) 478-2269
LOCATION: On S.R. 10 in Fort Gibson
OPEN: 9 A.M. to 5 P.M., Tuesday–Friday; 10 A.M. to 5 P.M., Saturday; and 1 P.M. to 5 P.M., Sunday; closed on Mondays and Oklahoma state holidays
ADMISSION: Free
FACILITIES: Visitors' Center with gift and book shop
HOTELS/MOTELS: Catalina Motel, 540 S. 32nd, Muskogee 74401, tel. (918) 682-3345; Quality Inn, 2300 E. Shawnee Ave., Muskogee 74401, tel. (918) 683-6551; Skylark Motel, 325 S. 32nd, Muskogee 74401, tel. (918) 682-7779; Holiday

Inn, 800 S. 32nd, Muskogee 74401, tel. (918) 682-4341
CAMPING: Webbers Falls Dam: Fort Gibson Park, Fort Gibson
74434, tel. (918) 489-5541; Webbers Falls Dam: Hopewell
Park, Muskogee 74401, tel. (918) 489-5541; Hilton's MHP, Rt.
3, Box 373, Muskogee 74401, tel. (918) 687-5055

History

Fort Gibson's history began in 1824 when Col. Matthew
Arbuckle, commanding five companies of the Seventh Infantry, selected a site on the left bank of the Grand (Neosho) River
to construct a military post. The decision to locate a U.S.
Army fort in the area was motivated by the massacre of a party
of white fur trappers on the Blue River in November 1823.
The fort, built under the direction of First Lt. Pierce M.
Butler, was named in honor of Col. George Gibson, Commissary General of Subsistence in the U.S. Army.

The first stage in Fort Gibson's history involves its role as a
peace-keeping military post in the Indian Territory. After Congress passed the Indian Removal Act in 1830, the troops
stationed at Fort Gibson played an important role in securing
peace in the Indian Territory that is now Oklahoma. President
Andrew Jackson's policy was designed to remove the Indian
tribes who lived east of the Mississippi River to locations west
of the river. Many of the eastern tribes were to be relocated to
the Indian Territory. This was particularly true of the "Five
Civilized Tribes" of the southeastern United States—the
Cherokee, Creek, Choctaw, Chickasaw, and Seminole.

The most poignant and tragic events of the forced exodus of
the eastern Indian tribes was the removal of the Cherokees on
what is called the "Trail of Tears." (For more information on
the removal of the Cherokees to Oklahoma, see the section on
Tsa-La-Gi and the Cherokee Heritage Center.) Once resettled
in Oklahoma, the five tribes reestablished their governments,
built towns, and founded schools.

The life-style of the eastern tribes sharply contrasted with that of the nomadic Plains Indians; and conflict erupted between the western tribes, particularly the Osage Indians, and the new arrivals from the east. In addition, there were also white intruders into what was to be the Indian's territory in perpetuity. The garrison at Fort Gibson now had the assignment of protecting the resettled Indians against raids by the Plains Indians as well as preventing incursions by white adventurers.

In 1831, Fort Gibson was made the headquarters of the entire Seventh Cavalry and then of the army's Department of the Southwestern Frontier. Its garrison was to explore the area and to act as a police force to prevent conflict between the western Plains Indians and the transplanted eastern tribes. It also served as a staging area for the transportation of the eastern Indians to the Oklahoma Territory. In 1836 when the resettlement of the Indians was completed, Fort Gibson was evacuated temporarily and its troops were ordered to the Texas border. In 1837 the post was reactivated and regarrisoned. In 1857 federal troops were withdrawn and the fort was turned over to the Cherokee Nation.

The second phase of Fort Gibson's history relates to the Civil War and post-Civil War reconstruction eras. When the Civil War began, the fort was occupied by Confederate troops. The Civil War had an impact on the Indian Territory in that the tribes were divided between supporters of the Union and the Confederacy. The Cherokees, in particular, were divided, with members of the tribe fighting on both sides and against each other.

On April 5, 1863, Fort Gibson was recaptured by Union troops, including some Cherokee volunteers, commanded by Col. William A. Phillips of the Indian Home Guard. The Union forces then erected fortifications on the hill above the old stockade area. Several new buildings and an extensive earthworks were constructed to defend the fort against a Confederate counterattack. After the Civil War ended, Fort Gibson continued to serve as an army post until its final evacuation in 1890.

The visitor to the site will actually see two forts. The log stockade and several of its outbuildings, which formed the original fort, were reconstructed in the 1930s by the Federal Relief Administration, the Works Progress Administration, and the Old Fort Gibson Stockade Commission. The second fort dates from 1845 when construction began on a new complex located on a hill northeast of the original stockade. Construction of the majority of the new fort's buildings took place between 1867 and 1871. Today the Fort Gibson Military Park is administered by the Oklahoma Historical Society. It should be noted that some of the fort buildings are also privately owned.

Tour

Fort Gibson, a military park maintained by the Oklahoma Historical Society, portrays the soldier's life on a U.S. Army post in the Indian Territory during the nineteenth century. The fort should appeal to travelers interested in military history and in historic restoration since the site contains some completely restored buildings as well as those that are being maintained to prevent deterioration. In addition, the military park contains archeological sites.

The **Stockade**, a large log rectangle enclosing an area 104 by 106 yards, was built from 1824–28. The reconstructed stockade, located 35 to 50 yards northeast of the original site, is a two-thirds-scale representation of the original fort. Within the stockade is a small **Visitors' Center** where a short slide presentation provides an overview of the fort's history. Visitors can then take a self-guided walking tour of the offices and quarters within the stockade.

The **Powder Magazine** is a separate stone building used to store cartridges and gunpowder.

The **Adjutant's Office and Bedroom** have whitewashed interiors with rooms outfitted with an army-issue desk, chair, and rope cot.

An **Enlisted Men's Quarters** contains four wooden cots and other furniture.

The **Officer's Quarters** contains an army kit on display, a rope bed, washstand, hour glass, and large desk chair.

An exhibit room in the stockade contains pictures and photographs of the Cherokee National Guard; Sam Houston, leader of Texas independence; Jefferson Davis, who visited the fort; Gen. Zachary Taylor; and Washington Irving, the author. At various times in its history, the fort was visited by these prominent individuals.

The second part of the tour takes the visitor outside the stockade to the new fort area, which consists of several restored buildings and archeological sites.

The ruins of the **first fort bakehouse** is an archeological site. Such bakehouses were important parts of military installations when the War Department recommended that the troops bake their own bread instead of purchasing it from outside bakers. The money saved was to be used for a fund for the troops.

The **company kitchens** are a row of buildings, constructed between 1832 and 1835, which provided the cooking facilities for the enlisted men. Since the army of the 1830s did not specifically designate men who were to be cooks, the enlisted men took turns in cooking for their companies. One of the buildings also has a large dining room with tables and settings of army-issue dishes and silverware.

The **Commanding Officers' Quarters** in the new section replaced the earlier quarters located within the stockade.

The **remains of the Civil War earthworks** represent the remnants of the 1,800 yards of earthern defenses erected by Union troops after they reoccupied the fort in 1863 during the Civil War.

The sites of the **Civil War Blockhouse,** the **Quartermaster**

Storehouse, and the Officers' Quarters mark the locations of fort buildings of the 1860s which no longer stand.

The large Barracks Building gives an excellent portrayal of the life of the enlisted men in the U.S. Army. Construction of the building, which began in 1845, went through a series of stages. In the late 1850s a part of the building was used for offices. During the reoccupation by federal troops in 1863, it was used as a lookout post and a storehouse. Construction of the barracks resumed in 1867 and was completed in the early 1870s. The interior of the barracks is white-washed with wide wooden plank floors. The large squadroom portrays the area where the enlisted men lived and slept. Wooden bunks, bedding, foot lockers, blue army uniforms, weapons, and polished boots are laid out for inspection. The dining area has tables set with army-issue tin cups and plates.

The Commissary Storehouse, built in 1848, was used to store the garrison's foodstuffs. In the mid-1870s, it was temporarily used as a barracks.

The Magazine, built in 1863 during the Civil War, was constructed of stone and slate and built within a hillside to make it fireproof and to minimize the dangers of an explosion.

A second post bakehouse, completed in 1871, supplied the garrison with bread.

Side Trips

The city of Muskogee has the following attractions: the U.S.S. Batfish, a World War II submarine, is permanently moored at War Memorial Park on the Arkansas River. The Five Tribes Museum contains artifacts and documents relating to the history of the tribes. The Thomas-Foreman Home, maintained by the Oklahoma Historical Society, was built in 1898 and is open to visitors.

Information on these and other area historical sites and recreational facilities is available from the Muskogee Tourist

Information, Rt. 3, Box 375G, Muskogee, OK 74401, tel.
(918) 682-6751. The center is open from 9 A.M. to 5 P.M.

Indian City, U.S.A.

Re-creation of Plains Indian villages

ADDRESS: Indian City, U.S.A., P.O. Box 695, Anadarko, OK
73005
TELEPHONE: (405) 247-5661
LOCATION: 2½ miles southeast of Anadarko, off U.S. 62
OPEN: Daily, 9 A.M. to 6 P.M. in summer; 9 A.M. to 5 P.M. in
winter
ADMISSION: Adults, $4; children 6 to 11, $2
FACILITIES: Guided tours, Indian dancing, craft shop, mu-
seum, American Indian Exposition, campground
HOTELS/MOTELS: Best Western Inn, 2101 S. 4th St., Chickasha
73018, tel. (405) 224-4890; Remington Inn, U.S. 81 and
H.E. Bailey Turnpike (I-44), Chickasha 73018, tel.
405-222-5050
CAMPING: Indian City, Thunderbird Campground, Box 695,
Anadarko 73005, tel. (405) 247-9043 or (405) 247-5661; Best
Western RV Park, Box 989, Chickasha 73018, tel. (405)
224-4890; Fort Cobb State Park, S.R. 146, Fort Cobb, tel.
(405) 643-2249

History

Named for the Nadarko band of Caddo Indians, Anadarko
was the location of several Indian agencies established for the
Caddo, Wichita, Delaware, Kiowa, Apache, and Comanche
tribes. Among the first to locate in the area were the Caddoes,

who settled in 1859 near the Washita River. In 1867 the Kiowas were resettled south of the river. In 1878 the various separate agencies were joined into a single office that still functions. Today, Anadarko is the location of Indian City, U.S.A., a corporation organized and owned by its citizens, and the place where the American Indian Exposition takes place each summer.

Dedicated in 1955, Indian City, U.S.A., located two and one-half miles southeast of Anadarko, is designed to preserve and exhibit the history of the American Indians. It is a recreation of seven Indian villages that are grouped into a single complex.

The American Indian Exposition, which features pageantry, dancing, and ceremonies, is held during the second week of August at Anadarko.

In microcosm, Indian City recaptures the larger history of the Indian Territory that is now part of Oklahoma. In the early nineteenth century, the U.S. government embarked on a policy to relocate the Indians who lived east of the Mississippi River to regions west of the river. In particular, the Indian Territory, which originally had been the tribal lands of the Wichita and the Kiowa, was divided into reservations and smaller tracts of land for the thirty-five tribes that were resettled in the area.

By the 1880s, the familiar pattern of encroachment of white settlers on Indian land was repeated. Whites were poised to occupy the Indian Territory that had been granted to the Indians in perpetuity. In 1887, Congress passed the Dawes Act which allotted each Indian listed on tribal rolls 160 acres of land. The remaining acreage, the major part of Oklahoma, was then opened to white settlers. In 1889 the famous "run" into Oklahoma occurred, and seventeen years later, in 1906, Oklahoma was admitted as a state.

Indian City, located on a 160-acre tract of the Kiowa, Comanche, and Apache reservations, is an outdoor museum that portrays the life of the American Indian by means of re-created villages. It is designed to provide a perspective into seven different Indian cultures. It should be remembered that the Native Americans were a people of many cultures rather than a single one. Although the Indian has often been stereotyped in novels and motion pictures, the Native Americans developed a wide variety of languages and cultures.

Each village depicts a different style of Indian life and culture that derived from that tribe's adaptation to the natural environment. For example, tribes that lived primarily by agriculture, such as the Pueblos and the Caddoes, resided in permanent villages. Hunting tribes, such as the Wichita, were nomadic and followed the herds of buffalo or other animals which were their source of food.

In visiting the Indian villages, visitors should remember that the dwellings are representative selections rather than an entire village. Thus, a village will be much smaller than it was in historical reality.

Each of the villages is outfitted with the artifacts of the particular tribe's material culture—the weapons, tools, pottery, musical instruments, and other items—that reflected the tribe's life-sustaining activities, such as farming or hunting. The nonmaterial aspects of the culture, such as religious ceremonies, social organization, and art forms, also reflected the means by which the tribe lived. In addition to the re-created villages, the Indian City Museum also has an extensive display of Indian artifacts.

Tour

The next section presents a historical sketch of each tribe whose village has been re-created at Indian City.

Kiowa Winter Camp

The Kiowas, who originally lived in the mountainous region of the upper Missouri River, migrated to the southwest and settled in what is now Oklahoma, Texas, Kansas, and

Colorado. They were skilled horsemen who were closely allied with the Comanches. Like other Plains Indians, the Kiowas followed the buffalo herds, which were their main supply of meat and hides. The Treaty of Medicine Lodge in 1867 located them on the Kiowa-Comanche reservation.

The Kiowa Winter Camp contains two large **tepees,** conically shaped tents, consisting of an animal-skin covering placed over a frame of poles, with a smoke hole at the top. A tepee was decorated with paintings that depicted various events in the life of the owner, such as victories won or the animal form of his guardian spirit.

Since the Kiowas were a nomadic tribe that migrated with its source of food, the tepee was especially appropriate as a portable home which could be transported from location to location.

Caddo Village

The Caddo Indians originally resided in settlements along the Red River Valley in Louisiana and Arkansas. By the end of the eighteenth century, warfare and disease had greatly reduced their population. In 1835 the Caddoes began the first of many moves when they ceded their lands in Louisiana to the United States government and relocated in Texas. In 1855, they were assigned to a reservation near the Brazos River. They were then relocated to Oklahoma in 1859. When the Confederate army occupied Oklahoma during the Civil War, the Caddoes, who supported the Union, fled to Kansas and Colorado. They returned to Oklahoma in 1872.

Since the Caddoes were an agricultural people who located in a particular place, their dwellings, of the wattle-and-daub type, were more permanent than those of the nomadic hunting tribes. Basically, a **wattle-and-daub house,** such as those in the Caddo Village, used a type of construction in which a pole framework was intertwined with branches, vines, and rushes and then covered with mud plaster.

In building their houses, they first erected an exterior framework of solid timbers, about eight feet in height. Two large center poles were then put into place, and a beam was laid across them to support the roof. The rafters which formed the roof were joined at the center and the walls. The roof was completed by running interwoven willow boughs over it. The remaining spaces were chinked with pieces of wood and brush. The walls were then plastered with a mud mixture to create an adobe exterior. Smoke from the cooking fire was allowed to escape between the thatched roof and the tops of the walls which remained uncovered.

In addition to the wattle-and-daub houses, the Caddo Village also has a large **council house** and a **community shelter.**
Wichita Village

The Wichita, a tribe related to the Caddoes and the Pawnees, originally ranged from the Arkansas River in Kansas to the Brazos River in Texas. The Wichita had contacts with both Spanish and French explorers. The tribe's population was greatly reduced by smallpox. In 1835, they signed a treaty with the United States government that relocated them to Indian Territory. Conflicts with Texans and Comanches and then with the Confederate army plagued the Wichitas. After the Civil War, they returned to their reservation on the north side of the Washita River.

The Wichita Village includes a council house, a typical house, and a community shelter. The 40-foot-high **council house,** built of split pine poles set in the ground and joined at the top, is covered with willow branches and swamp grass. The **community shelter** was used for drying meat, vegetables, and curing buffalo hides.

In constructing the **Wichita house,** eight large cedar poles are set upright in a circle, spaced according to the size of the house. Rafters are laid across the tops of these upright poles, and cedar side poles are set in place. Four of these split side poles are placed to form a circle exterior to that formed by the eight main uprights. These four poles are then fastened at the top to form the conical shaped house. Willow branches are then strung around the exterior of the house. Swamp grass is used to thatch the house, and a smoke hole at the top provides for the elimination of smoke.

Chiricauhua Apache Village

The Chiricauhua Apaches originally inhabited south-western New Mexico, southeastern Arizona, and southern Mexico. Their first contact with the whites was with Francisco Vasquez de Coronado, the Spanish explorer, around 1540. A nomadic tribe, the Apaches raided other tribes for food and slaves and then continued this practice against the whites. The Apaches carried on guerrilla-like warfare against the Spanish, and then the Mexicans, and finally against the Americans. In 1861 the U.S. government began a twenty-five year campaign against the Apaches. In particular, the Chiricauhua Apaches were skilled desert warriors, led by such chiefs as Cochise, Mangas Coloradas, Victorio, and Geronimo. This tribe skirmished with and often eluded the Mexican and the American armies. The Apache Wars ended when Geronimo surrendered to Gen. Nelson A. Miles in 1886. The tribe was then forcibly exiled to Florida, where it remained until 1894 when its members were permitted to return to Fort Sill in Oklahoma. In 1913 the majority of the tribe took up residence in New Mexico. A minority, however, remained in Oklahoma in the vicinity of the town of Apache.

The Chiricauhua Apaches were organized into bands which were divided into local groups, consisting of from ten to twenty households or extended families. The Apaches lived by hunting, food-gathering, and raiding for food, horses, cattle, and slaves.

At Indian City, the Chirichua Apache Village, contains six **wickiups,** beehive-shaped dwellings of poles, brush, and grass, which were sometimes covered with skins. The wickiup frame is made of willow poles tied together at the dome. This frame is then covered with willow branches, grass, and yucca leaves. The entrance to each house is protected from the wind by an extension. The interior has grass beds. In the summer, cooking was done outside and in the winter on a small pit in the center of the wickiup. One of the wickiups is a steam lodge used by the men of the tribe for bathing.

Navajo Village

The Navajos are an Athapascan-speaking tribe related to the Apaches. The Navajo tribal lands were located in the Southwest between the Rio Grande, San Juan, and Colorado rivers. Originally a hunting and raiding tribe like the Apaches, the Navajos made a major change in their style of life when they began to herd sheep. As a pastoral people, they also developed handicraft and farming skills. They have become known for their jewelry and rugs.

The Navajos experienced conflicts with the white settlers. In 1863 an expedition led by Kit Carson defeated the Navajos. The following year United States Army troops forced 2,400 Navajos on the "Long Walk," a trek across 300 miles of New Mexico to Bosque Redando during which 200 died. The initial exiles at Bosque Redando were joined by 5,000 of their tribesmen. Because of its isolation, infertile soil, and desolation, Bosque Redando was disastrous for the Navajos. After vowing never to wage war again, the Navajos were allowed to return to their homeland in 1868.

The basic Navajo encampment consisted of an extended family, which was organized around a woman, her husband, their unmarried children, and their married daughters, their husbands, and unmarried children. Each household in the camp had its own hogan, or dwelling. However, farming, herding, and hunting were shared by the entire extended family.

The Navajo Village at Indian City consists of three **hogans** which illustrate two different styles of construction. One, resembling a beehive, is constructed of pine logs laid horizontally in a circular crisscross pattern and then plastered with adobe clay. The other two hogans illustrate more contemporary building methods in which pine timbers are set in the ground horizontally in a circle. There is also an outdoor baking oven.

Pawnee Village

The Pawnees, a tribe whose language was related to the Caddoes, were located in Nebraska's Platte River Valley. As was true of many Indian tribes in the region, the first contact with whites occurred when they encountered the Spanish explorer, Francisco Vasquez de Coronado. The Pawnees, like other Great Plains tribes, became horse-mounted at the end of the seventeenth century when they obtained horses from the southwestern nomadic tribes who had obtained them earlier from the Spanish.

After the Louisiana Purchase, the Pawnees had greater contacts with the American whites. In particular, their skill as horsemen made them sought after as scouts for the U.S. Army cavalry. They also acted as guides for railroad work crews when the transcontinental railroads were being built. The Pawnees' traditional enemies were the Sioux.

The Pawnees were a tribe that was generally friendly to the whites. Their contacts with the whites also exposed them to epidemic diseases to which they had little or no natural immunity. In 1831 a serious smallpox epidemic wiped out half the tribe. In 1849 a cholera epidemic further depleted the Pawnee population. In 1876 the remnants of the tribe moved to Indian Territory after ceding the last of their Nebraska lands to the United States.

The highly permanent Pawnee villages consisted of earth lodges, a man-made, dome-shaped dugout. The Pawnee Village at Indian City contains two such **earth lodges**. These dugouts consisted of a circular excavation, four feet in depth, with huge timbers placed in a circle in the center of the hole. Rafters were then placed across the tops of the center posts and peripheral beams were then set in place. Over a system of supporting beams and rafters were placed willow saplings. The structure was then covered with sod. White settlers in Nebraska often used sod houses also. The center area of these lodges was used for cooking, and the far end of the lodge for religious ceremonies. The outer wall of the lodge has a two-foot-high ledge for sitting and sleeping.

Pueblo Village

Most of the Pueblo Indians continue to live in their ancestral tribal lands in New Mexico, where the pueblos of Taos and Sante Fe are the oldest and most representative communities. The Pueblos, an agricultural people, had their first contacts with whites when they encountered the Spanish explorers and conquistadores.

Pueblo, meaning village in Spanish, refers to both the style of architecture and to the Indians who lived in them. The pueblo was a multistoried stone and adobe apartment-like structure with contiguous flat roofs. The only entry was through the roof, which was reached by ladders that could be pulled up in the event of an enemy attack.

Most of the Pueblos were dry-crop farmers, growing corn, beans, squash, and pumpkins. They were also skilled in such crafts as weaving, pottery-making, and jewelry-making.

The **pueblo** at Indian City is a singular illustration of what is in historic reality a large community. In the communities in New Mexico, such as that of Taos, a pueblo consists of clusters of adobe structures build around a square. Most pueblos also have an adobe church, a kiva, a cellar-like ritual chamber for ceremonial rites, and large, outdoor beehive-shaped adobe ovens.

Side Trips

The **Southern Plains Indian Museum,** Anadarko 73005, tel. (405) 247-3424, is devoted to the arts and crafts of the Plains Indians. Tours are available.

The **Anadarko Philomathic Museum,** located in the Rock Island Railroad Depot, preserves artifacts of pioneer and Indian life.

The **American Indian Hall of Fame for Famous American**

Indians is three blocks east of the junction of S.R. 8 and U.S. 62 East.

The **Wichita Mountains Wildlife Refuge,** one hour south of Anadarko, contains buffalo, longhorn cattle, deer, and elk.

Tsa-La-Gi

Re-creation of Cherokee Indian villages of the 1650–1700 period and 1880-1890 period

ADDRESS: P.O. Box 515, Tahlequah, OK 74464
TELEPHONE: (918) 456-6007
LOCATION: Between I-40 and I-44, 60 miles east of Tulsa, on U.S. 62
ADMISSION: Since Tsa-La-Gi is a complex of historical attractions, admission fees and times of operation for each are different.

CHEROKEE NATIONAL MUSEUM AND RURAL MUSEUM VILLAGE:

OPEN: Summer schedule: 10 A.M. to 8 P.M., Monday–Saturday; 1 to 6 P.M., Sunday. Winter schedule: 10 A.M. to 5 P.M., Monday–Saturday; 1–5 P.M., Sunday. Closed New Year's Day, Thanksgiving, Christmas Eve, and Christmas Day.
ADMISSION: Adults, $2.50; children 6–12, $1.25

ANCIENT VILLAGE:

OPEN: Daily, May 13–August 23, Monday–Saturday, 10 A.M. to 5 P.M.; Sunday, 1–5 P.M.
ADMISSION: Adults, $3.50; children, $1.75

THEATER AT TSA-LA-GI:

OPEN: Nightly except Sunday, June 6–August 22, performances at 8:30 P.M.

ADMISSION: Adults, $8; children, $4
ADDRESS: Trail of Tears Drama, P.O. Box 515, Tahlequah, 74464, tel. (918) 456-6007

NOTE: A package ticket is available for theater, Cherokee National Museum and Rural Village, and Ancient Village: Adults, $12; children, $5.50.

FACILITIES: Cherokee National Museum, gift shop, theater
HOTELS/MOTELS: Tsa-La-Gi Lodge, P.O. Box 948, Tahlequah 74465, tel. (800) 831-9640
RESORT: Western Hills Guest Ranch, Sequoyah State Park, Box 509, Wagoner 74477, tel. (918) 772-2545; Tenkiller State Park, Star Route, Box 169, Vlan 74962, tel. (918) 489-5641
CAMPING: Lake Fort Gibson, Box 370, Fort Gibson 74434, tel. (918) 687-2167; Tenkiller State Park, Star Route, Box 169, Vlan 74962, tel. (918) 489-5643; Sequoyah State Park, Rt. 3, Box 112, Hubert 74441, tel. (918) 772-2046

History

Tsa-La-Gi is a memorial to the history of the Cherokees. Along with the Creeks, Choctaws, Chickasaws, and Seminoles, the Cherokees were one of the "Five Civilized Tribes" who lived originally in the southeastern United States. Before the Europeans arrived in North America, the Cherokees occupied about 40,000 square miles in the southern Allegheny region, which is now comprised of southwest Virginia, western North and South Carolina, northern Georgia and Alabama, and eastern Tennessee. Today, only a small number of Cherokees remain in the eastern United States.

Although the Cherokees encountered Spanish and French explorers and traders, their greatest contact was with the English. Intermarriage between British traders and Cherokee women produced mixed-blood families bearing such names as

Adair, Lowry, Rogers, Ross, Vann, and Ward. Certain of these mixed bloods became prosperous merchants and planters.

In the colonial period of the late 1700s and the early 1800s and during the early American republic, cessions of land to white settlers reduced the Cherokee tribal lands to the southern Appalachians of western North and South Carolina, northern Georgia and Alabama, and eastern Tennessee. Between 1794 and 1819, land cessions between the U.S. government and the Cherokee Nation reduced tribal lands to half their original size.

As their tribal region became smaller, the Cherokees were more determined to preserve their way of life. They believed, however, that they could adopt some political and educational processes from the whites and still maintain their Indian cultural identity. For example, a number of Cherokees became prosperous farmers and merchants but continued to hold their land in tribal ownership.

Foremost, the Cherokee leaders believed that their survival depended on education. Influenced by Christian missionaries such as Samuel A. Worcester, they built schools and churches. Some mission school graduates attended academies and colleges in New England. As a result, the Cherokee Nation developed a cadre of educated leaders including John Ross, Elias Boudinot, Stand Watie, John Ridge, and Charles Hicks.

In 1832, Sequoyah completed his Cherokee alphabet, an eighty-five-character system, which rendered the Cherokee language into written form. Sequoyah's alphabet made the Cherokees a literate people, the first Indian tribe to have a written language. Written communication advanced further in 1828 when Elias Boudinot began publishing the *Cherokee Phoenix*, a bilingual English and Cherokee newspaper.

In 1827 at a convention at New Echota, the Cherokees adopted a constitution patterned after the U.S. Constitution which established a two-house legislature, a supreme court, a jury system, and a national police force. John Ross was elected principal chief.

Despite the economic, political, and educational achievements of the Cherokees, their vision of a peaceful and prosperous Cherokee Nation was soon reduced to ashes. White settlers, hungry for land, were poised to occupy the Cherokee land.

Some Cherokees had already left their tribal lands. Between 1808 and 1817, some 2,000 Cherokees, yielding to the pressure of white settlers, moved voluntarily from the Southeast to a reservation in northwestern Arkansas. Between 1817 and 1819, an additional 4,000 tribesmen ceded their lands to the U.S. government and moved to Arkansas. By the late 1820s an official policy of the U.S. government was emerging that all Indians who lived east of the Mississippi River were to be removed to the territories lying to the river's west. In 1828 the 6,000 Cherokees who had earlier relocated in Arkansas signed a treaty with the U.S. government which ceded their lands in return for a 7-million-acre tract in the Indian Territory, now part of northeastern Oklahoma.

Unrelenting pressure was mounted against the approximately 18,000 Cherokees who remained in the East. At the urging of President Andrew Jackson, who as a general had led several military campaigns against the Indians, Congress passed the Removal Bill, which empowered the president to exchange land west of the Mississippi for territory held in the East. Although the U.S. Supreme Court upheld the right of the Cherokees to their southeastern lands, President Jackson, refusing to enforce the court's ruling, ordered the army to forcibly remove the Cherokees.

Along with anti-Cherokee pressure from the Jackson administration and land-hungry white settlers, the Georgia legislature, through a series of laws, claimed jurisdiction over the Cherokee land and divided it into lots to be sold to white settlers. The legislature further denied the right of Cherokees to testify in court against whites and cancelled any debts which whites might owe to them.

U.S. government policy for the removal of the Cherokees caused dissension and factions to develop within the tribe. Convinced that they had no choice but to leave, a Treaty Party led by Major Ridge, John Ridge, Elias Boudinot, and Stand Watie urged signing the treaty that would cede their land. However, John Ross, principal chief of the Cherokees, adamantly opposed the treaty.

In 1835, members of the Treaty Party signed a secret treaty with the U.S. government ceding all Cherokee lands east of the Mississippi and agreed to move to the Indian Territory. Between 1835 and 1838, 2,000 Cherokees identified with the Treaty Party left for the Indian Territory. Ross, the leader of the majority of the Cherokees, claimed the treaty was invalid and refused to join the exodus to the West.

In May 1838, federal troops, commanded by Gen. Winfield Scott, occupied the Cherokee Nation. Driving the Cherokees from their ancestral lands, the army forced them to march westward. During this trek, known as the "Trail of Tears," several thousand Cherokees perished because of cold, hunger, and disease.

When the resettlement was completed, conflicts arose between the "Old Arrivals," the Cherokees who had migrated earlier from Arkansas, and the "New Arrivals," the eastern Cherokees. Complicating the internal conflict was the presence of the Treaty Party members who had allied with the "Old Arrivals." Seeking revenge, a group of "New Arrivals" assassinated several of the leaders of the Treaty Party whom they held responsible for the tribe's plight.

Unity was restored on July 12, 1839, when, under the leadership of John Ross, an Act of Union was adopted to unite the contending factions. This was followed by the adoption of a new constitution, signed on September 6, 1839, at Tahlequah, the new capital of the Cherokee Nation. In 1846 a treaty signed between the Cherokees and the U.S. government guaranteed the Cherokee title to their lands in the Indian Territory. From 1840–61 the transplanted Cherokees created a prosperous and orderly society.

Especially important to the cultural revival of the Cherokees after their removal to the Indian Territory was the Park Hill Mission, founded in 1836 by Rev. Samuel A. Worcester, a Presbyterian missionary. Worcester also established the Park Hill Press, a bilingual English and Cherokee press, that published selections from the Bible, textbooks, and the *Cherokee Almanac*. In 1851, two secondary schools were established. The Male Seminary and the Female Seminary were both three-story classical brick structures staffed by teachers from eastern colleges. Fire destroyed the Female Seminary in 1887 and the Male Seminary in 1910.

Like the rest of the United States, the Civil War had an impact on the Cherokee Nation. In 1861, Principal Cherokee Chief John Ross negotiated an alliance with the Confederacy. In 1862, Union and Confederate armies fought for control of the Indian and Oklahoma Territories. The victorious Union army occupied these territories. Once again, the Cherokee Nation was weak and divided.

After the Civil War, the frontier of white settlement pushed relentlessly westward. Once again, white settlers were poised to occupy the land of the Indian Territory, which was opened to homesteaders in 1889. The Oklahoma Territory was organized in 1890, and its population grew so rapidly that in 1907 the Oklahoma and Indian Territories were admitted into the Union as the state of Oklahoma in 1907. Today, Tsa-La-Gi stands in testimony to the Cherokee Nation, which numbers 100,000 persons in the United States, 25,000 of whom live in Oklahoma.

Tsa-La-Gi, the Cherokee Heritage Center, was established in 1963 by the Cherokee National Historical Society, a private nonprofit organization chartered to preserve the history of the

Cherokee people. Tsa-La-Gi is a complex which includes two museum villages, the Ancient Village and the Rural Village, as well as a museum, library, theater, and chapel. After several years of planning, construction of the center began on the site of the Cherokee Female Seminary, which from 1851–87 was one of the important educational institutions in the West and one of the earliest colleges for women west of the Mississippi River. Three brick columns that remain of the seminary building, destroyed by fire in 1887, are the symbols of the center.

The first phase of construction saw the creation of the Ancient Village. Cherokee craftsman, using native building materials and ancient methods, re-created the village which depicts life before the coming of the Europeans to North America. The Ancient Village was opened to the public in 1967. The second phase was completed when the Theater at Tsa-La-Gi opened in 1979 with the first performance of the drama "Trail of Tears." The third stage of development was completed in 1975 with the opening of the Cherokee National Museum, which includes the outdoor Rural Village, opened in 1980.

Tour

The **Ancient Village of Tsa-La-Gi**, 1650–1700, portrays tribal life before the coming of the Europeans. Designed as a living historical experience, the Ancient Village re-creates Cherokee life in the southern Appalachians from 1650–1700, when the eastern Cherokees, a woodland people, lived by hunting, fishing, and primitive agriculture. The village is the size of an average settlement of 200 persons.

The village, protected by a log stockade, contained food stores and an internal water source, a necessity in the event of an enemy siege. A narrow passageway, allowing entrance by one person at a time, provided access.

Village society was organized by membership in one of the seven large clans of the tribe: Wolf, Deer, Bird, Paint, Blue, Wild Potato, and Twister.

A guided tour visits the dwellings. Craft demonstrations feature beadworking, basket-making, and pottery-making.

The **Cherokee National Museum, Archives, and Library** provides visitors with the story of the Cherokee people through displays of art, crafts, artifacts, and other exhibits. Designed by Charles C. Boyd, the museum, a structure of concrete and steel faced with native sandstone, is based on the Cherokee log house. Ramps and facilities are provided for handicapped visitors.

The **Adams' Corner Rural Village** recaptures life in the Cherokee Nation from 1875–90, the period preceding Oklahoma statehood. When put in perspective with the Ancient Village, the visitor can experience the development of the Cherokee Nation. The Ancient Village portrays life as the Cherokees lived it in their ancestral home in the southeastern part of the country before the coming of the whites. The Rural Village carries the story forward in time to the late nineteenth century and to the American West, where the Cherokees adapted to a new and different environment.

Swimmers School, a one-room country school, with a steepled bell tower, features a classroom equipped with late nineteenth-century books, such as *McGuffey's Readers*, and other educational materials. The schoolyard has a water pump and a seesaw. The school was constructed from materials from the old Stapler Mansion built in 1880.

The **Smith General Store,** a stocked general store and post office, was also constructed from materials from the Stapler Mansion. The store carried items which could not be produced at home; its porch was often a gathering place for informal meetings.

The **Community Church,** a log structure with handmade pews, also has a Sunday School classroom. Dating from 1870, the building was moved to its present location from the south edge of Tahlequah.

The **Log Cabin,** dating from 1870, was moved to the site from Lost City. It depicts the home of the small farmer and trapper.

The **white frame house** portrays the dwelling of a prosperous Cherokee family. It contains a fireplace from the Keener Vann home.

The **Theater at Tsa-La-Gi** attracts thousands of visitors each year to see the epic drama *Trail of Tears*, which portrays the plight of the Cherokee who were forcibly removed from their ancestral home in Georgia and North Carolina and by forced march were resettled in the Indian Territory that is now eastern Oklahoma. Through song, dance, and drama, the pageant portrays the tragic exodus, the travail of resettlement in a strange land, and the eventual triumph of the Cherokees in Oklahoma. The drama unfolds against the national backdrop of such major events as the Civil War and Oklahoma's admission to statehood in 1907.

The **Ho-Chee-Nee Memorial Prayer Chapel,** designed by Charles Chief Boyd, fulfills the dream of Mrs. Jimalee Burton, Ho-Chee-Nee, a Cherokee artist, poet, and writer. Mrs. Burton's small, stone, nondenominational chapel stands as a memorial to those who perished on the Trail of Tears.

The chapel's symbolism is both artistic and mystical. Architecturally, the chapel integrates the style of the ancient Cherokee council house with contemporary religious symbols. The three massive vertical poles on the east symbolize the Trinity. The seven poles on the roof symbolize the seven Cherokee clans. The altar's motif uses Cherokee pottery designs.

The **Cherokee Arboretum and Herb Garden** includes species of plants used by the Cherokees for food, fiber, and medicines.

The **Cherokee Wild Life Refuge** at Tsa-La-Gi contains buffalo and deer.

Side Trips

The town of Tahlequah, settled by the transplanted eastern Cherokees, contains several historical sites. Tahlequah, the name of the Cherokee capital, meaning "two is enough," is based on the decision of two of three members of a Cherokee delegation to locate the capital at this location. Tahlequah became the official Cherokee capital in 1839. Today, the city of 12,000 is the location of several significant historical buildings.

The **Old Seminary Hall,** built in 1889, replaced the burned Cherokee Female Seminary. It is located on the Northeastern Oklahoma State University campus.

The **Murrell Home,** a southern-style mansion, constructed in 1844 by George M. Murrell, a wealthy Cherokee merchant, has been restored by the state of Oklahoma. It is located one-half mile south of the main entrance to Tsa-La-Gi.

The **Cherokee National Capitol,** a two-story brick structure located in the middle of the town square, was built in 1869. It served as the Cherokee Nation's capitol and then as the Cherokee County Courthouse. Under restoration, it is located at the 100 block of S. Muskogee Ave. It is designated as a National Landmark.

The **Cherokee Supreme Court Building,** of 1844, located to the southeast of the capitol building, is listed on the National Registry of Historic Sites.

The **Cherokee National Prison,** built in 1874, served as a prison until 1907. It is listed on the National Registry of Historic Sites.

Will Rogers Memorial, W. Will Rogers Blvd., Claremore, houses the effects, manuscripts, and tomb of the Oklahoma-born American humorist. It is open daily from 9 A.M. to 7 P.M.

National Cowboy Hall of Fame is located at 1700 N.E. 63 St., Oklahoma City. It is open daily from 8:30 A.M. to 6 P.M.

Sequoyah's Home is located in Sequoyah's Cabin State Park, on S.R. 101, 10 miles northeast of Sallisaw. It preserves on its original site the cabin built by Sequoyah, the inventer of the Cherokee alphabet in 1829. It features documents and artifacts associated with Sequoyah.

9

TEXAS

Lyndon B. Johnson National Historical Park and Lyndon B. Johnson State Historical Park

Restoration and preservation of sites related to Lyndon B. Johnson, thirty-sixth president of the United States

LYNDON B. JOHNSON NATIONAL HISTORICAL PARK:
ADDRESS: P.O. Box 329, Johnson City, TX 78636
TELEPHONE: (512) 868-7128
LOCATION: The Johnson City sites are located in Johnson City at the intersection of U.S. 290 and 281; the LBJ Ranch Unit is 22 miles from Johnson City on U.S. 290.

OPEN: Daily, 8 A.M. to 5 P.M.; closed on Christmas. (Note: the National Park tour bus which leaves from the State Park Visitors' Center operates from 10 A.M. to 4 P.M.)
ADMISSION: Free
FACILITIES: Tour bus to LBJ Ranch unit, gift shop

LYNDON B. JOHNSON STATE HISTORICAL PARK:
ADDRESS: Box 238, Stonewall, TX 78671
TELEPHONE: (512) 644-2252
LOCATION: At Stonewall, entrance from U.S. 290 East
OPEN: Daily, 8 A.M. to 5 P.M.; closed Christmas Day
ADMISSION: Free
FACILITIES: Gift and book shop, swimming pool, pavilion, children's wading pool, tennis courts, picnic areas
HOTELS/MOTELS: Holiday Inn-North, 6911 N. Interregional Hwy. (I-35), Austin 78752, tel. (512) 459-4251; Best Western Chariot Inn, 7300 N. Interregional Hwy. (I-35), Austin 78752, tel. (512) 452-9371
CAMPING: Pedernales Falls State Park, Rt. 1, Box 31A, Johnson City 78636, tel. (512) 868-7304; KOA Madison Hill Country, Rt. 1, Box 238, Fredericksburg 78624, tel. (512) 997-4796; Roadrunner Travel Park, Box 217, Johnson City 78636, tel. (512) 868-7449

History

The Lyndon Baines Johnson National and State Historical Parks commemorate the Texas years of Lyndon B. Johnson, the thirty-sixth president of the United States. These historical parks are located in the "Texas Hill Country," a region that lies between the more humid coast area and the drier high plains. It was in the hill country that Samuel Ealy Johnson, Lyndon's grandfather, and his great uncle, Jesse Thomas Johnson, settled in the 1860s and worked as cattle ranchers. The Johnson family prospered and rose to social and political prominence in the Texas hill country. Johnson City is named for James Polk Johnson, a nephew of Sam Johnson.

Samuel Ealy Johnson, Jr., the son of Sam Johnson and father of Lyndon Johnson, carried on the family business and traditions. A well-known rancher and local politician, he married Rebekah Baines, a well-educated young lady from the town of McKinney. Sam Johnson, Jr., served in the state legislature where he supported liberal legislation designed to improve the condition of the farmers and ranchers who were his constituents.

Lyndon Baines Johnson, the oldest of their five children, was born near Stonewall, Texas, on August 27, 1908. The future president's early life was associated with the hill country sites preserved in the two parks. In 1913, when Lyndon was five, the Johnson family moved to Johnson City. Lyndon attended local schools and graduated from Johnson City High School in 1924. He attended Southwest Texas State Teachers College at San Marcos and majored in history. After receiving his B.S. degree in 1930, he taught public speaking and debate at Sam Houston High School in Houston.

On November 17, 1934, Lyndon Johnson married Lady Bird (Claudia Alta) Taylor of Karnak, Texas. Mrs. Johnson was the daughter of a Texas planter and merchant. The Johnsons had two daughters, Lynda Bird and Luci Baines.

Like his father and grandfather, Lyndon B. Johnson was attracted to politics and a career in public service. He began his career as a public official during the New Deal when he was appointed in 1935 as state director of the National Youth Administration for Texas.

In 1937, he was elected to the U.S. House of Representatives and re-elected for five terms, serving until 1948 when he was elected to the U.S. Senate. During World War II, he served in the U.S. Navy as a lieutenant commander while on a leave of absence from Congress. Johnson became one of the most powerful and influential members of the Senate in which he served as Democratic leader.

The senator from Texas sought the Democratic nomination for president in 1960 but was defeated by John F. Kennedy, who then chose him as his vice-presidential running mate. Kennedy and Johnson were elected. When President Kennedy was assassinated in Dallas, on November 22, 1963, Johnson became president. He was re-elected in 1964, defeating Senator Barry Goldwater, the Republican candidate.

Johnson's presidency was known for his Great Society programs designed to advance voting rights and civil rights, eradicate poverty, and promote equal educational opportunity. His administration was marred by the intense national division that was caused by the increasing United States' involvement in the conflict in Viet Nam. He declined to be a candidate for the presidency in 1968, informing the nation in a televised speech that he would not accept the Democratic nomination for president.

Lyndon Johnson died on April 8, 1972, of a heart attack in Charlottesville, Virginia, and is buried in the Johnson family cemetery on the banks of the Pedernales River.

Tour

The National and State Historic Parks should each be viewed as telling an important and related part of the Texas history of Lyndon Johnson. The Texas Parks and Wildlife Department operates the state park located across the Pedernales River from the LBJ Ranch. The National Park Service administers sites on the opposite side of the Pedernales River and within Johnson City. Together these parks interpret the Texas hill country, its impact on Lyndon Johnson, and his career as senator and president.

The Lyndon Johnson National Historical Park contains sites

in two separate areas: Johnson City and the LBJ Ranch. A Visitors' Center provides information about these sites and their locations.

In Johnson City, the principal sites are the **Boyhood Home of Lyndon Johnson** and the **Johnson Settlement.** The Johnson family moved to the future president's boyhood home in 1913 when Lyndon was five years old. He lived in the family home until he graduated from college in 1930.

The eight-room frame house has been restored to the 1920 time period. In the home's interior are the hallway which also served as the private office of Lyndon's father, Sam E. Johnson, Jr., who was a politician, member of the Texas legislature, and a real estate and insurance agent. The girls' bedroom was shared by Lyndon's three sisters, Rebekah, Josefa, and Lucia; it is decorated in the style of the 1920s with two beds, dressers, and a sewing machine. The dining room, the most used room in the house, was the scene of family gatherings. Its large table and chairs and other furnishings are period pieces. The parlor, a room reserved for formal occasions, is furnished in the formal style and furniture of the times. The large master bedroom was used by Johnson's parents. The simply furnished boys' bedroom was shared by Lyndon and his brother Sam. The baseball, bat, and glove, while not Lyndon Johnson's own, are exhibited to demonstrate his love of the national pastime. The tub room was added in 1922. The kitchen with cast-iron stove, table, and cabinets was a modern kitchen of the 1920s. The sleeping porch was used during the hot summers.

The **Johnson Settlement,** a complex of restored structures, traces the development of the Texas hill country from the early 1860s when it was dominated by large open-range cattle ranches to the more local ranching and farming of the contemporary era. The **Exhibit Center** has displays that portray the transition of the hill country from open Texas range land to smaller farms and ranches.

Among the structures in the Johnson Settlement are the **Johnson Headquarters,** a log cabin that was the headquarters of Thomas and Sam Johnson's cattle-driving operations. Between 1867–72 the cabin was a rendezvous point for the individual ranch owners who would bring their cattle to the Johnson brothers for the long drive to the Kansas railroads.

The **James Polk Johnson Barn,** was purchased by James Polk Johnson, Sam Johnson's nephew in 1872. It portrays the transition which James made from cattle drover to rancher.

The **James Polk Johnson House,** a two-story frame home and smoke house, was built in 1882. Johnson was the founder of Johnson City, for whom the settlement was named.

The **Bruckner Barn** was built in 1882 on land that was sold by James Polk Johnson to John Bruckner, a German immigrant. This large stone barn is constructed according to German design.

Access to the **LBJ Ranch,** which is a working ranch, is exclusively by tour bus operated by the National Park Service. Tour buses leave from the State Park Visitors' Center. The ranch tour includes the restored **one-room country school** attended by Lyndon B. Johnson, the **Johnson Family cemetery,** and views of the ranch.

The Lyndon B. Johnson State Historical Park is located directly across from the LBJ Ranch and contains a **Visitor's Center,** which features exhibits and memorabilia on Johnson's boyhood and youth, and photographs of the presidential years and of distinguished visitors to the ranch. It also has exhibits on the Texas hill country and its early settlers, especially the various ethnic groups who located in the region.

The **Behrens Cabin,** a two-room dog trot cabin built by the German immigrant Johannes Behrens in the 1870s, is furnished with period pieces. It is attached to the Visitors' Center.

The State Park also contains the **Sauer-Beckmann Farmstead,** an operating historical farm which has been restored to depict life and agriculture in the year 1918. Docents perform farm chores and conduct tours.

Also in the park are a nature trail, a hill country botanical exhibit, and wild life enclosures stocked with bison, white-tailed deer, wild turkeys, and longhorn cattle.

Side Trips

The **Lyndon B. Johnson Library and Museum,** 2313 Red River St., Austin, TX 78705, tel. (512) 482-5279, is located one block west of I-35. Open daily from 9 A.M. to 5 P.M., it is located on the campus of the University of Texas at Austin and is operated by the National Archives and Records Service of the General Services Administration. It is an archive for manuscripts and documents related to the career of President Johnson. It also houses a museum that has extensive exhibits on Johnson's long career as a public servant.

San Antonio Missions National Historical Park and San Antonio de Valero Mission (The Alamo)

Four original early 1700s Spanish missions; National Register, National Historic Landmark. An original early 1700s Spanish mission, commonly called the Alamo, that was the site of the famous 1836 battle of the Texas Revolution; National Register, National Historic Landmark

ADDRESS: National Historic Park, 2202 Roosevelt Avenue, San Antonio, TX 78210; Mission Concepcion, 807 Mission Rd.; Mission San Jose, 6539 San Jose Dr.; Mission San Juan, 9101

Graf Rd.; Mission Espada, 10040 Espada Rd.; the Alamo, P.O. Box 2599, Alamo Plaza, San Antonio, TX 78299

TELEPHONE: National Historic Park: (512) 229-5701; the Alamo: (512) 222-1693

LOCATION: In the city of San Antonio, along the San Antonio River

HOURS: National Historic Park: daily 8 A.M. to 5 P.M. during Central Standard Time and 9 A.M. to 6 P.M. during Daylight Saving Time; closed Christmas and New Year's Day; the Alamo: open Monday to Saturday, 9 A.M. to 5:30 P.M., Sunday, 10 A.M. to 5:30 P.M.

ADMISSION: Free; donations accepted

FACILITIES: Interpretive museum at Mission San Jose; interpretive centers at Mission San Juan and Mission Espada; eight-mile hike-bike trail

HOTELS/MOTELS: Marriott, 711 E. River Walk, San Antonio 78205, tel. (512) 224-4555; Hyatt Regency, 123 Losoya, on the River Walk at Paseo del Alamo, San Antonio 78205, tel. (512) 222-1234; St. Anthony Intercontinental, 300 E. Travis, San Antonio 78205; Menger Hotel, Alamo Plaza, San Antonio 78205, tel. (512) 223-4361 and (800) 345-9285; La Mansion Del Rio, 112 College St., San Antonio 78205, tel. (512) 225-2581

CAMPING: Hidden Valley Campground, 207 Sunny Creek, San Antonio 78228, tel. (512) 623-9898; Kampground 6/Dixie, 1011 Gembler Dr., San Antonio 78219, tel. (512) 337-6501; Yogi Bear-San Antonio, 2617 Roosevelt Ave., San Antonio 78214, tel. (512) 532-8310; Roosevelt Avenue MHP, 700 N. St. Mary's, San Antonio 78205, tel. (512) 534-8215

History

Spain was the leading European power in the early imperial rivalry for North America. Between 1513, when Ponce de

Leon discovered Florida, and 1821, when a newly independent Mexico assumed control of Spanish possessions in the present United States, Spain was dominant in the Southeast and Southwest, particularly in the present states of Florida, Texas, New Mexico, Arizona and California.

Spanish motives for colonization were to locate mineral wealth, to convert the Indians to Christianity and to block French and English efforts to take over their claims. The Spanish method of colonization was the mission system in which armed forces established forts or presidios while missionaries converted the Indians to Catholicism and taught them agricultural techniques, trades and crafts of Spanish civilization.

The Spanish mission system in North America began in the 1500s and lasted until the early 1800s. The first area colonized by Spain was Florida in the sixteenth century, then New Mexico in the late sixteenth century. Texas was the third major area followed by California.

The threat of losing territory to the French was the impetus for Spanish settlement in Texas. The French explorer, Rene Robert Cavelier, Sieur de la Salle, claimed the Mississippi River system for France in 1682, naming it Louisiana. When in January 1685, La Salle, along with three ships and their crews overshot the Mississippi River by 400 miles and landed at Matagorda Bay, on the east coast of Texas, the Spanish, who learned of it from coastal Indians, became concerned. They regarded it as a French attempt to take over Spanish territory. Their fears intensified when they heard that La Salle had built a fort, Fort St. Louis.

The Spanish decided to locate and destroy this French fort and colony, sending excursions by both land and sea. When Captain Alonso de Leon located the colony in 1689, it was deserted. De Leon burned the fort to the ground, thus wiping out any trace of French occupation in the area. La Salle had been murdered by his own followers.

The following year a priest who had traveled with De Leon's party, Father Damien Massanet, founded a mission in east Texas among the Tejas or Texas Indians, after whom the state was named. Mission San Francisco de los Tejas, the first Franciscan mission in Texas, was begun at the invitation of the friendly, highly civilized Tejas. The mission was short-lived however. An epidemic struck the mission Indians during the winter of 1690–91 killing 3,000—half of their number. The natives associated the deaths with the baptismal rites performed by the padres which they saw as mysterious and evil. Because of their fear, the Indians became uncooperative and the mission was abandoned in 1692.

Father Francisco Hidalgo, one of the priests who served at Mission San Francisco de las Tejas, worried about those Indians who had remained faithful Christians. Although he sent repeated pleas to reestablish the mission, the Spanish crown ignored him. In 1711, after 19 long years of frustration with Spanish authorities, Father Hidalgo wrote to the French governor of Louisiana at Mobile on the Gulf Coast asking him to cooperate in establishing a mission among the Texas people. Agreement by the French would involve their entry into Spanish territory which the Spanish vehemently opposed.

The French were delighted with the invitation. Although their concern for Indian souls was minimal, their desire for acquisition of more French territory and for opportunities to trade French goods for Spanish silver was very strong. Governor Cadillac appointed Louis Juchereau de St. Denis, a Canadian who was a former officer in the king's army, and also an explorer and Indian trader who had excellent relationships with the Caddo, Yatasi and Natchitoches Indians, to lead the expedition. Cadillac provided St. Denis with a passport to which he attached the letter of invitation to the French from Fr. Hidalgo.

In September 1712, St. Denis entered New Spain accompanied by 24 men and carrying a huge amount of goods to trade. After traveling by water as far as the Red River, Natchitoche Indian territory, St. Denis built warehouses to store his goods. The site of the warehouses became the first permanent center of white settlement in the present state of Louisiana. St. Denis and his party then marched on and located the Indians. They remembered Father Hidalgo and expressed a wish that he return.

Next, St. Denis traveled to the Spanish mission and presidio on the Rio Grande, Mission San Juan Bautista and Presidio del Rio Grande. The Spanish were astonished by the appearance of the French expedition in their territory, and despite St. Denis' explanation that he was merely looking for Father Hidalgo, he was put under house arrest until orders about his disposition came from authorities.

Thirty-eight-year-old St. Denis was, by all accounts, an exceptional man, possessed of charm, good looks, and the rare ability to get along with all kinds of people. He was particularly well-known for his friendly relations with the Indians. His success was based on his ability and willingness to adapt to the Indian lifestyle rather than trying to change it like most other Europeans. Even his house arrest at the Spanish mission was friendly, and no doubt the commandant and St. Denis probably engaged in mutually profitable, though illegal, trading.

While under arrest, St. Denis fell in love with the commandant's 17-year-old granddaughter, Manuela Ramon. His rival, Don Gaspardo Anza, governor of Coahuila, ordered that St. Denis be brought in chains to Mexico City to explain his actions to the viceroy. But, Anza's power was no match for the charm and abilities of St. Denis. Things did not go quite the way Anza had planned. Although it was abundantly clear that St. Denis had improperly entered Spanish territory, his excellent skills as an explorer and map maker were quickly recognized by the Mexico City officials.

The conclusion was that the Spanish government saw it was

in their interest to reestablish the Tejas mission requested by Padre Hidalgo. In fact, the Spanish authorities decided that four, maybe even six, missions should be started in the Texas region. Domingo Ramon, son of the commandant at Presidio del Ros Grande and uncle of Manuela Ramon, was named commander of the entrada and St. Denis, the French prisoner, was hired as the conductor of supplies at a salary of 500 pesos.

While the supplies and personnel for the entrada were being organized, St. Denis traveled ahead to Mission San Juan Bautista de Rio Grande to marry Manuela. The Spanish viceroy presented the French groom with a wedding present of 1,000 pesos and a bay horse and provided an escort of 10 soldiers. The wedding of this extraordinary Frenchman and his Spanish bride took place in the spring of 1716.

By that time, the 75-man entrada was complete. It was composed of Franciscan priests, Indian guides, Spanish soldiers and a long pack train loaded with tools, weapons, food, religious items and livestock including goats, sheep, oxen, horses and mules. When the Spanish entrada reached the Texan camp, it was warmly received. The site for San Francisco de las Tejas was on the Neches River, west of the original mission. Padre Hidalgo was put in charge.

A second mission named Nuestra Senora de la Purisma Concepcion was established near a Hasinai village. Nine miles southeast, Father Margril and Captain Ramon started a third mission, Nuestra Senora de Guadalupe, in a Nacogdoches village. The fourth mission, 15 miles northeast of Mission Purisma Concepcion, was in a Nasini village and was named Mission San Jose. These simple missions usually consisted of a small log church with a hut nearby for the priests.

The new missions were not successful for a variety of reasons. Spanish motives for the founding of these missions had more to do with demonstrating their claim to the region and preventing French encroachment on it than saving Indian souls. Although missions were not founded without the permission of the local Indians, most were not committed to

Christianity. Inevitably, the natives resented the changes imposed by the padres and the punishments received for violating mission rules.

Not long after the Texas missions were founded, the padres were pleading for more supplies and more soldiers and a presidio to protect them. Their requests were delivered to the new viceroy, Marquis de Valero, in Mexico City by Father Olivares in late 1716, who also asked for an additional mission and presidio on the San Antonio River. This request was granted and the mission was established in May 1718. Named San Antonio de Valero, the adobe mission on the San Antonio River had a presidio nearby named San Antonio de Bexar. This mission was destined to be famous, but would be known by another name: The Alamo.

Meanwhile, in the war that raged in Europe in 1718 with Spain and France on opposite sides, ramifications were being felt in the North American colonies. In June 1719, Lt. Blondel from the French fort at Natchitoches arrived at Mission San Miguel de los Adaes with orders to seize all Spaniards. A lay brother who managed to escape alerted neighboring missions and the Spaniards retreated to Mission San Antonio de Valera with its nearby presidio for protection from the French.

Spain responded to the French threat by sending the newly named governor and captain-general of Texas, Marques de San Miguel de Aguayo, to reoccupy the territory and drive the French back to Louisiana. Aguayo's huge entrada wasn't ready until 1721, by which time the European war had ended. St. Denis, who was the commander of the French troops at Natchitoches, and Aguayo met and agreed to abide by the European truce. However, Aguayo did reestablish the abandoned missions. Despite protests from St. Denis, Aguayo also established a presidio at Los Adaes which was inside the Louisiana border and only a few miles away from the French settlement of Natchitoches. For half a century, the presidio served as the capital of New Spain's province of Texas.

In 1720, Father Margil organized a new mission under the sponsorship of Marquis Aguayo after whom it was named—Mission San Jose y San Miguel de Aguayo. In January 1722, Aguayo returned to the presidio of San Antonio de Bexar to supervise the construction of a new presido. It consisted of a square adobe fort with two bastions built on the west bank of the San Antonio River. Inside the walls were a church, a powder magazine and barracks constructed of wood. The misssion retained its original name: San Antonio de Valero. Aguayo then erected a mission and a presidio on the site of the French Fort St. Louis which had been burned by De Leon 30 years before.

When Aguayo left Texas in 1727, there were four presidios, nine missions and small clusters of settlers at San Antonio and Los Adaes. Between 1724 and 1727, the presidios of New Spain's long northern frontier were inspected by Brigadier Pedro de Rivera, the viceroy's visitador, to find ways of cutting military expenses. One of his suggestions was to abandon the oldest presidio in Texas, Nuestra Senora de los Dolores de los Texas, thus forcing the removal of the three east Texas missions under its protection.

The closed missions were relocated on the San Antonio River, not far from Mission San Antonio de Valera and the presidio at Bexar, in 1731. Working among the Coahuiltecan Indians proved more successful than the missions had been in east Texas.

San Francisco de los Texas was renamed San Francisco de la Espada, San Jose de los Nazonis was renamed San Juan Capistrano, and Nuestra Senora de la Purisima Concepcion de los Hasinai was changed to Nuestra Senora de la Purisima Concepcion de Acuna. The five missions along the San Antonio River were the nucleus for the present city of San Antonio.

In 1761, Spain acquired western Louisiana from France, and Mississippi became the eastern frontier of New Spain. Much of the settlement of Texas had resulted from Spanish fear of French encroachment. With the removal of the French threat, Spain decided to abandon all Texas missions and presidios except those at San Antonio and La Bahia in 1773.

The San Antonio missions were towns built like walled fortresses for protection against Apache Indians who had become more active after some of the Spanish presidios had closed. Franciscan priests taught their formerly nomadic charges who had hunted and gathered their food to farm and tend livestock. Construction skills like stonecutting and brick laying were also taught as Indian labor replaced the original adobe buildings with impressive stone structures in the 1740s. Indians also constructed the excellent system which irrigated the fields of the five missions.

Each mission became a thriving community which was home to hundreds of Christian Indians. The prosperity of the missions was partially based on large herds of cattle. In 1778, the Spanish authorities declared that all unbranded cattle were government property, which dealt the missions a significant economic blow.

The end of the eighteenth century was a time of decline for the San Antonio missions. Factors included diseases which proved fatal to large numbers of Indians, raids by hostile Apaches and the partial secularization of the missions in 1794. At that time, mission lands were distributed among the remaining Indians and some missions became submissions of others. Although churches continued to function, the Franciscans left when the Mexican government, now independent from Spain, in 1824 completely secularized the missions which became deserted.

As the Anglo population of Mexican-held Texas grew due to white immigrants from the eastern United States during the 1820s, increased pressure mounted for Texas to become an independent state, free of Mexican rule. Mexico's response was to pass the Law of April 6, 1830, which forbade immigration into Texas by U.S. citizens. Stephen Austin, leader of the colonization of Texas, appealed to Mexican authorities to repeal this law, which they did in December 1833. However, Austin did not persuade President Santa Anna that Texas should be independent. In January 1834, Austin was arrested on suspicion of trying to incite insurrection in Texas and imprisoned for over two years accelerating the deterioration of relations between Texas and the Mexican government.

The Texas Revolution broke out in September 1835 with the goal of reinstating the liberal Constitution of 1824, although the underlying goal of independence from Mexico quickly emerged. In response, a brother-in-law of Mexican President Santa Anna, General Martin Perfecto de Cos, and an army of 500 men, moved into San Antonio to expel all Anglo settlers, who had arrived since 1830, and arrest Texas revolutionaries.

Stephen Austin appointed Ben Milam and a company of scouts to determine the best way to assault San Antonio. Milam and 300 men attacked San Antonio on December 5, 1835, and the battle with Cos raged for three days. Although Milam was killed, the Texans drove the Mexicans back. On December 10, Cos signed a capitulation giving the Texans all public property, money, arms and ammunition in San Antonio. Cos agreed to withdraw south of the Rio Grande and not fight the Texans again. This seemed to mark the end of the war, but Santa Anna wanted revenge.

In 1836, Santa Anna set out for San Antonio. Just outside the city was the abandoned mission of San Antonio de Valero, known as the Alamo for a nearby grove of cottonwood trees, alamos. Mexican forces had occupied this mission until General Cos removed his troops from the city.

On February 23, 1836, the day General Santa Anna arrived in San Antonio, Colonels William Barret Travis and James Bowie occupied the Alamo with approximately 145 men. The following day, 5,000 Mexican troops began a siege on the Alamo. Inside, Bowie was incapacitated by typhoid-pneumonia and Travis was in command. David Crockett and some of his Tennessee Boys, who had joined the fight for Texas independence were also inside.

For 13 days, the Alamo was under siege. Santa Anna called for unconditional surrender. The courageous Texans answered with a cannon shot and vowed never to surrender. Although Travis repeatedly sent messengers out of the fortified mission with appeals for help, only 188 Texas troops defended the Alamo. After March 3, no one entered or left the fort. Legend has it that on that day, with all hope gone, Travis drew a line across the dirt floor and invited all who would stay and die with him to step over the line. All the men stepped over the line with the exception of Jim Bowie who asked that his cot be carried over the line.

On March 6, at 4 a.m., the Mexican assault on the mission began with waves of soldiers equipped with picks, spikes and scaling ladders attacking the walls from the north, the east, the south and the west. Texas gunfire pushed the Mexicans back twice. On their third attack, they concentrated on the battered north wall. Climbing over the parapet into the plaza, they engaged the courageous Texans in hand-to-hand combat. By 8 a.m., every Texas soldier lay dead. Mexican losses have been estimated at close to 1,000.

Under orders from Santa Anna, Mexican troops built a giant pyre of wood and dead bodies. It was set on fire before dusk.

The extraordinary bravery and heroism of the Texas troops at the Alamo became the inspiration for other Texans in the fight for freedom. "Remember the Alamo" became their rallying cry. Six weeks after the Alamo defeat, at the Battle of San Jacinto under the leadership of Sam Houston, Santa Anna was captured, and the Mexican army surrendered. Texas gained its freedom from Mexico.

In 1983, four of the five missions in San Antonio became the San Antonio Missions National Historical Park under the supervision of the National Park Service. The Alamo became an outdoor museum operated by the Daughters of the Republic of Texas and the State of Texas in 1905.

Tour

The missions of San Antonio are a part of what makes San Antonio a treasure, a city rich with Spanish architecture and history built along the picturesque San Antonio River. Early eighteenth-century Franciscan missions make an outstanding contribution to the flavor and atmosphere of this unique Texas city.

Located along a seven-mile section of the San Antonio River, the missions are accessible from Mission Parkway. Traveling from north to south along Mission Parkway, the order of the missions is 1) Mission San Antonio de Valero, the Alamo, 2) Mission Concepcion, 3) Mission San Jose, 4) Mission San Juan, and 5) Mission Espada. The Espada Aqueduct is also a part of the National Historical Park.

Mission San Antonio de Valera, known to us today as the **Alamo,** combines Texas' Spanish colonial heritage with a shrine to the heroes of the Texas revolution. It is often referred to as "The Cradle of Texas Liberty."

The history of the Alamo goes back almost 300 years to the establishment of the Franciscan mission by Father Antonio de Olivares in 1718. The original mission complex which consisted of between two and three acres contained a church and a large, two-story stone structure called the Long Barrack. This building contained living quarters for the priests, offices, a dining hall and kitchens.

What remains of the mission today are the low gray chapel, which is renovated and maintained as an historic shrine, the ruins of two living quarters and some crumbling, ivy-covered walls.

Work on the existing stone church, which has been restored, began in 1744. Destroyed by a storm a few years later, the chapel was rebuilt. Poor construction caused a partial collapse and it was never completed.

Mission buildings, left vacant after the mission was abandoned, became a convenient shelter for military troops. Spanish troops were the first to take advantage of the empty buildings. Mexican General Cos quartered his troops there in 1835 when he was sent to quell the revolutionaries in San Antonio. Cos was defeated and moved his troops out of the mission.

When General Santa Anna decided to win back San Antonio, it was Texas troops who holed up in the mission. After a 13-day siege, thousands of Mexican soldiers stormed the mission killing all 188 Texans inside. The Battle of the Alamo marked a turning point in the Texas fight for freedom. The Alamo heroes became the inspiration for other Texans who soon accomplished their goal.

The Alamo remains as the symbol of freedom in Texas and has become a shrine. The U.S. Army repaired the mission buildings in 1849 and completed the unfinished chapel facade. The State of Texas purchased the chapel in 1883 and the Long Barrack in 1905. The property was placed in the custody of the Daughters of the Republic of Texas and they maintain it as a shrine and museum. The story of the Alamo is recounted through exhibits in the chapel and in two museums.

The Long Barrack, which was begun in 1727, is now a museum with exhibits on the Alamo and the history of the Republic of Texas. Two dioramas depict the Battle of the Alamo. The Alamo Museum displays historical portraits, documents, manuscripts, guns, coins and other items associated with the history of Texas and the Alamo. Souvenirs and books are sold here. Also on the grounds are the lovely Convent Garden and a wishing well. The Texas History Library of the Daughters of the Republic of Texas contains books, documents, maps, manuscripts, and art works relating to Texas history.

Nuestra Senora de la Purisima Concepcion de Acuna,

known as **Mission Concepcion,** is the oldest unrestored stone Catholic church in the United States. The mission was moved from its original site 300 miles east in 1731 and located on the banks of the San Antonio River, Spain's northern frontier.

Although the mission was once a complex of buildings including stone houses, classrooms, shops and a granary, today only the church and a L-shaped convento remain. The church, which is completely original, was dedicated on December 8, 1755.

The stuccoed limestone church was constructed on bedrock which is one explanation for its survival. Built in Mexican Baroque style, the church is in the traditional Latin cross shape, and has twin, massive bell towers with belfries. The entrance decorations include a pediment with a circular window above it, columns and relief carvings.

Traces of the original frescoes painted in natural plant and mineral colors can be seen in the barrel-vaulted nave. A fresco of the "Eye of God" is visible on the ceiling of a room in the convento.

The mission was secularized in 1793. It was occupied by the U.S. Army in 1849. In 1887 it was returned to the church and is still a parish church today with frequent religious services. It is administered under a cooperative agreement between the National Park Service and the Catholic Archdiocese of San Antonio as a parish church and an historical site.

San Jose y San Miguel de Aguayo Mission, known as **Mission San Jose,** was founded in 1720 by Padre Antonio Margil de Jesus who had established the east Texas missions of Dolores, Guadalupe and San Miguel, all closed by Spanish officials in 1720. Margil named the mission on the San Antonio River in honor of Marques de San Miguel de Aguayo, Governor and captain-general of Texas.

At its height during the mid-eighteenth century, there were approximately 200 Coahuiltec Indians living at the mission.

Its fields produced 3,000 bushels of corn annually, and its herds included 2,000 cattle and 1,000 sheep.

Flooding and other natural calamities necessitated moving the mission locally several times. The first buildings were of adobe. In 1739, at its present location, stone structures were built. The present church was begun in 1768 and completed in the 1770s. Other mission structures included Indian quarters, barracks, a mill, a granary, shops and storerooms.

Mission San Jose is often described as the most beautiful mission in Texas, and was called the queen of all missions in New Spain. Its reputation for beauty is based on its original facade richly decorated in a Renaissance style, and its exquisite Rosa's Window. This window has the flowers and fruits of the pomegranate carved around it. The oft-copied window has been credited to either master mason Antonio Salazar or Pedro Huizar. Legend has it that the artist carved the window in memory of his lost love, Rosa.

Mission San Jose was secularized in 1794 and its farmlands were distributed to the 78 remaining mission Indians. The last Franciscan priest left in 1824. During the nineteenth century, the mission fell into disrepair. The dome and roof of the central church fell in.

In 1917, funds were raised to preserve the convento, the church and the granary. During the 1930s, the Works Progress Administration rebuilt much of the original compound. In 1937, the church was rededicated. The mission became a Texas state park in 1941 and in 1978 became a part of San Antonio Missions National Historical Park.

In addition to the church, the Roman and Gothic arches of the two-story convento remain as does the restored granary. Thousands of bushels of corn were stored inside its 600-foot-long walls. The restored granary is one of the oldest stone structures in San Antonio, and is noted for its flying buttresses and vaulted roof.

You may tour the Indian quarters which are built around the walls of the missions. Each small stone apartment housed an Indian family. The flour mill was built in 1790. The second floor is a restoration while the grinding room on the first floor is original.

Mission San Juan Capistrano, known as **Mission San Juan**, was founded in east Texas in 1716 and moved to the banks of the San Antonio River in 1731. The first order of business in the new location was to plant fields and dig irrigation ditches. Ranching was based 30 miles away at Rancho San Rafael de Pataquilla where there were 1,000 cattle and 3,500 sheep.

Mission buildings made of adobe with thatched roofs were erected as temporary shelters. Later construction was of stone. The present church, built in 1767, is a rectangular building of rubble construction. The side walls of the church feature segmented arches between buttresses. A two-tiered, three-arched bell tower is one of the building's most prominent features.

Mission San Juan looks today almost as it did when the priests left. The site includes the restored church, convent, and several houses. Other buildings are in ruins or have been partially excavated. Much of the original courtyard has been preserved. The cells in the outer walls remain as they were when Indians and soldiers lived there.

Partial secularization was ordered in 1794. The Indians would take over the farms and herds. No priests were to remain at Mission San Juan and the mission would become a visita (sub-mission) of Mission Espada. In 1824, Mexico, now independent of Spain, completely secularized the mission. Buildings fell into disrepair. In 1886, the church roof was destroyed in a storm and was not repaired until 1909. The mission was restored by the Archdiocese of San Antonio during the 1960s. Today San Juan is a parish church and a part of San Antonio Missions National Historical Park.

Mission San Francisco de la Espada, known as **Mission**

Espada, is located on the edge of the city of San Antonio. Its remoteness gives you a feel for the isolation and self-sufficiency that was the reality of mission life.

Of the original mission complex, the site now includes the small, reconstructed chapel, the facade of which is original, the kitchen and dining room of the convento, and the low foundation of the surrounding walls, a granary and a fortified tower. The mission complex was arranged to form a traditional quadrangular courtyard.

Twenty-five miles south was the mission ranch, Rancho de las Cabras, where 4,000 sheep and 1,200 head of cattle were raised.

The small, rectangular chapel is noted for its unusual facade which features a three-bell espadana and trefoil arch. Inside the church are some of the original hand-carved, primitive wooden statues of saints. They have flexible joints and glass eyes. Mission Espada is a parish church and services are held regularly.

Espada Aquaduct is located about one mile north of Mission Espada between it and Mission San Juan. Still operating, the irrigation system was built by mission Indians under the direction of the Franciscan friars between 1731 and 1740.

Side Trips

Spanish Governor's Palace was the residence and headquarters of eighteenth-century Spanish governors and vice governors of Texas. Built in 1749, it is the only remaining example of a Spanish colonial dwelling in Texas. The walls of this authentically restored plastered adobe building are three feet thick. Ceiling beams are hand hewn and some rooms have their original native flagstone floors. The ten rooms of the palace are furnished with antique Spanish furniture. At the rear of the building is a patio with cobbled walks, a fountain, and gardens planted with native flowers and shrubs. It is located at 105 Military Plaza, San Antonio, TX 78205; tel. (512) 224-0601; open Monday–Saturday, 9 A.M. to 5 P.M., Sunday, 10 A.M. to 5 P.M.; guided tours only; Adults, $.75, children, $.25; closed holidays.

River Walk, Paseo del Rio runs for several miles through the heart of San Antonio along the San Antonio River and is one of the most delightful attractions of the city. The walk is lined with tropical foliage and sidewalk cafes and is a great place for strolling.

La Villita, bounded by Paseo de la Villita, South Presca, South Alamo and Nueva Streets, is a group of restored nineteenth-century buildings. Shops specializing in arts and crafts, restaurants and museums occupy the buildings. Open Monday through Saturday; tel. (512) 299-8610.

HIPPOCRENE U.S.A.

Also by the Guteks

EXPLORING THE AMERICAN WEST: A GUIDE TO MUSEUM VILLAGES

Covering California, Arizona, New Mexico, Colorado, Wyoming, Oregon and Washington, "this is a wonderful source of historical information...a gold mine for travelers. Highly recommended."– *Literary Journal*

213 pages   ISBN 0-87052-793-2   11.95 paper

EXPLORING THE BERKSHIRES

Herbert S. Whitman, illustrated by Rosemary Fox

"This gem of a book with delightful pen-and-ink drawings... has lots of local lore."– Conde Nast's *Traveler*

240 pages   ISBN 0-87052-516-6 $9.95 Paper

Also by the same author and artist

EXPLORING NANTUCKET

A charming introduction to North America's most elusive and exclusive vacation spot. "Anyone contemplating a visit to the island would benefit from this book."–ALA, *Booklist*

120 pages   ISBN 0-87052-792-4 $14.95 paper

AMERICA'S HEARTLAND

Tom Weil

Weil charts the less-trodden by-ways and hidden corners of Illinois, Indiana, Iowa, and Missouri, relating them to the history of the region.

423 pages   ISBN 0-87052-748-7 $14.95 paper

Also by Tom Weil

AMERICA'S SOUTH

In the only single-volume guide covering 11 southern states, Weil seeks out the eccentricities and less known attractions of Dixie.

423 pages   ISBN 0-87052-611-1 $14.95 paper

HIPPOCRENE U.S.A.

THE SOUTHWEST: A FAMILY ADVENTURE
Tish Minear and Janet Limon
The national parks and historic sites of the Colorado Plateau
are a natural museum for kids. This imaginative book details
itineraries through Utah, Arizona, Colorado and New Mexico, with plenty of advice on how to take your family on the
road in the desert and still stay cool!
456 pages   ISBN 0-87052-640-5 $14.95 paper

THE GUIDE TO BLACK WASHINGTON: PLACES AND
EVENTS OF HISTORICAL SIGNIFICANCE IN THE NA-
TION'S CAPITAL
Sandra Fitzpatrick and Maria Goodwin
288 pages   ISBN 0-87052-832-7 $14.95 paper

LONG ISLAND: A GUIDE TO NEW YORK'S SUFFOLK
AND NASSAU COUNTIES
Raymond, Judith, and Kathryn Spinzia
Covers over 430 historic, cultural, recreational and en-
vironmental sites, and lists all the Tiffany windows located
in the region.
284 pages   ISBN 0-87052-555-7 $14.95 paper